CARLOS ESPINAL

Fundraising Field Guide v3

A Startup Founder's Handbook

First published by Reedsy 2024

Copyright © 2024 by Carlos Espinal

All rights reserved. No part of this publication may be reproduced, stored or transmitted in any form or by any means, electronic, mechanical, photocopying, recording, scanning, or otherwise without written permission from the publisher. It is illegal to copy this book, post it to a website, or distribute it by any other means without permission.

Third edition

Proofreading by Kate McGinn & David Ola
Proofreading by Millan Suri & Daniel Inge
Proofreading by Will Bennett & Amber Patel

This book was professionally typeset on Reedsy. Find out more at reedsy.com

Contents

Donations for Cause — v
Foreword — vi
Introduction to the Third Edition — viii

I Part 1 — Looking for Investment

1. Planning for Fundraising — 3
2. Preparing Your Company for Fundraising — 13
3. Round Sizing: Further Implications — 36
4. The Fundraising Process — 40
5. Your Fundraising Materials — 47
6. The Power of Storytelling — 67
7. The Human Element — 74
8. The Search for an Investor — 82
9. Managing Your Fundraising Process — 115

II Part 2 - Closing Your Investment

10. Understanding Your Deal — 125
11. Understanding Valuation — 146
12. Toxic Rounds — 166
13. Managing the Legal Process — 178
14. Conclusion — 191

III Appendix — Additions to the First Edition

15 Get Your Elephant in the Room Under Control!	195
16 Weatherproofing Your Startup for any Financial Climate	198
17 Deciphering Crowdfunding	204
18 Additional Resources	211
Acknowledgments	214
How This Book Was Made	218
About the Author	220

Donations for Cause

Thank you for reading, buying, or gifting this book.

I believe everyone with the ambition, drive, and desire to change their life for the better should have that opportunity.

In that spirit, I've been working with Resurgo Spear, on supporting their Spear Programme.

To learn more about them and to make a donation to support their efforts, please visit Resurgo's website:

https://resurgo.org.uk/spear-programme/the-spear-programme/

If you enjoy this book or received it as a gift, please consider sharing it with friends and donating the suggested sum of $/£10.99 or more to the charity listed on this book's website:

http://www.fundraisingfieldguide.com

Additionally, please consider leaving a review on whichever platform you purchased the book from!

Foreword

Yes, the sweetest monies a startup can ever see in their bank account are those paid by their customers. Alas, few brand new companies (especially in tech) bootstrap to this moment on founder's own capital alone. You need investors to front the bills before you can take care of it yourself.

We've seen many fellow founders get stuck on the most obvious, yet not the most important, things about fundraising, like, say, valuation. In reality, much more innocent-looking nuances, such as board composition or liquidation preferences, might dictate your company's eventual outcome more.

The fact that Carlos gets to talking about the alphabet soup of specialized term sheet legal buzzwords only about 100 pages into the book shows you how thoughtful and systematic he is, first unpacking the entire logic and life cycle of funding companies across many years, understanding the philosophy and incentives of people involved, and guiding on how to avoid common pitfalls.

If you are not lucky enough to have Carlos and Seedcamp as your partners yet (you should!), reading this book is the next best thing to calling him up for advice.

Sten Tamkivi (Plural, Skype, Teleport) & Taavet Hinrikus (Plural, Wise, Skype)

***

As founders, we've experienced the difficulties of the fundraising process first-hand.

As investors, having participated in more than two hundred deals via LocalGlobe, we have experienced close-up many of the challenges that early-stage founders go through, and observed many of the patterns of what it takes to succeed as well.

The purpose of this book is to help founders streamline their learning process around how fundraising works. While fundraising isn't rocket science, it does involve its own vocabulary, and relies heavily on relationships, careful preparation, courage and lots of patience.

Through his experience at Seedcamp and his previous role as a venture capitalist (VC), Carlos has highlighted many of the important points to consider while fundraising.

Robin & Saul Klein, LocalGlobe

Introduction to the Third Edition

Since 2007, I've been fortunate to participate and invest in over three hundred startup journeys at every stage of development, from generating an idea to finding product-market-fit to raising investor money, and finally to scaling operations and exits. During this time, I've reviewed hundreds of cap tables, countless financial growth and hiring plans, and lived through some tough emotional discussions with founders, the topics of which range from their very personal health and family issues to inter-founder disputes due to the stress of startup life.
These cumulative experiences have given me a certain viewpoint on startup life—a perspective on the bravery and courage many founders have when embarking on their entrepreneurial journeys, and the seemingly uncertain and almost random way growth events can unfold during a company's life. Many of the chapters in this book are based on real-life stories of founders I've worked with, and how they overcame key challenges at various steps of their journey.

Many of the chapters of this book originally started as posts on my blog, The Drawing Board, which I created in an attempt to help new founders avoid the pitfalls I have witnessed others struggle through. I approach the effort of observing and recounting the lessons I've learned over the years with the humility of a student. I believe it takes a beginner's mindset and an ever-learning ethos to successfully tackle the constantly and rapidly evolving nature of startup life. In that spirit, when this book was first published in 2016 it contained the core of what I had learned about fundraising up to that point. However, all things and ideas evolve with time.

This edition includes all the useful information of the original but also brings things up to speed with how fundraising has evolved as of 2023/2024. Ask any writer or creator what they think of their work, and I suspect many will say they feel like they are never done. That's exactly how I feel about this book. Every year, I learn something new that I wish to incorporate into a new edition so that it is even more up-to-date, but, as with most things in life, there has to be a "good enough" point for it to be complete. I feel, revising this book for its third version has captured a very interesting period which marks the completion of a full cycle of fundraisings for startups.

The First Edition of the *Fundraising Field Guide* was written during the 'fast linear' growth curve of the post-2007/8 crisis period. The second edition was produced during the bubble formed in Covid when large injections of capital into private markets led to an exponential growth period for startups and their valuations. When I wrote the second edition of the book, there were a few chapters I was hesitant to update with revised advice because of what I suspected would happen — which is what we are seeing now (end of 2023)— namely, the compression of valuations due to inflated rounds driven by excessive investor greed and fear of missing out (FOMO) exacerbated by some of the cheapest capital available in human history. This third edition tackles all of that and more. Below I highlight the major changes in the VC landscape I've observed in the eight years between the first and third editions of this book:

- Success of VC as an asset class leading to the entry of many new investors into the previously local ecosystems, including the arrival of many foreign investors seeking price arbitrage from their home markets
- The collective drive to find companies that could generate returns that exceeded normal exit multiples, thus forcing growth strategies that were unsustainable.
- The emergence of many unicorns as a function of capital injections driving valuations over created value
- The creation of specialized investors across the different stages of financing, all the way through to IPO, due to the speed at which people could make money at even the latest of stages
- Added pressure on founders to tell compelling stories that could justify the massive expectations from all investors across their growth journey
- Increasing round sizes to have a 'war chest' to compete against other startups tackling the same kind of ideas
- Competition between investors on financing terms and structures vs value add leading to disproportionate increases in valuations as round sizes grew larger and investors competed to win by trying to appear more founder friendly,
- The removal of many tried and true governance terms as part of investment rounds leading to a variety of misbehavior by many, both investors and founders
- Greater expectations for pay, perks, options, etc. from

startup employees with little loyalty to the company, leading to further pressure on founders to adapt how they play to win
- The rise of remote-first companies that brought with them many complications (as well as benefits)
- Positive changing attitudes to tech entrepreneurship in Europe (risk and failure is OK!) which has thankfully continued
- The creation of the 'Platform VC' approach driving VC to be have more like a product
- "Celebritization" of VC's (e.g. PG, Andreessen, The Chainsmokers, Ashton Kutcher, Nico Rosberg, etc.) and an overlap with other popular culture (e.g. Sir Mike Moritz co-authoring a book with Sir Alex Ferguson)

As you can see from all the change that happened in a relatively short period of time above, no one strategy functions consistently well forever. I also don't think any one way or framework can possibly contain the myriad challenges a founder encounters during their journey. My hope, as you read this edition of the book, is that you approach what I've written in this book with the same mentality: taking it as a direction, if you will, but not a fixed one. When thinking about the elements discussed in this book and how they apply to you, consider them in the context of where you are in the business cycle. For example, in times when capital is plentiful, you might be able to lean in on elements that are more about your long- term vision and narratives. But, when capital is scarcer, you'll likely need to supplement with more facts and figures and with a more sustainable growth strategy, depending on the stage your company is in. The point is — adapt.

There is so much I have learned from the founders I've worked with. I hope you find this book as useful and interesting as my work with them has been. It's their stories and experiences that have enabled this book to happen.

With that in mind, I also encourage you to talk about what you get out of this book with other founders because, it is in the spirit of communal discussion that I've seen the best ideas surface.

Note: Throughout this book, I use examples which include numbers/figures that aren't designed to be recommendations or representations of what's "market standard" for investors or founders. Some of these numbers, I suspect, will age badly, as inflation erodes their relative value. As we will cover in the section on milestones and valuations, so much depends on the type of business you are creating, where you are fundraising, and the current macroeconomic climate. I also do not set out to comprehensively discuss all forms of fundraising instruments, such as traditional debt instruments, to name one. Rather, the book focuses on financings typical of early-stage, high-growth companies, and as such, covers mainly fixed- and variable-price structures.

I
Part 1 — Looking for Investment

"Perseverance is not a long race; it is many short races one after the other."
– Walter Elliot

1

Planning for Fundraising

The Tao of Fundraising

There is a Taoist story of an old farmer who had worked his crops for many years. One day, his only horse ran away. Upon hearing the news, his neighbors came to share his sorrow. "Such bad luck," they said. The farmer replied, "Good news, bad news—just the same."

The next morning, the horse returned, bringing with it three other wild horses. "How wonderful," the neighbors exclaimed. "Good news, bad news—just the same," replied the old man.

The following day, the farmer's son tried to ride one of the untamed horses, was thrown, and broke his leg. The neighbors again came to offer their sympathies at his misfortune. "Good news, bad news—just the same," came the familiar reply.

The day after that, military officials came to the village to draft young men into the army. Seeing that the farmer's son's leg was broken, they passed him by. The neighbors congratulated the farmer on how well things had turned out.

"Good news, bad news," said the farmer, "just the same."

All fundraising efforts and meetings have a elements of good news and bad news. How you deal with them and learn from them is what really matters.

The Fundraising Mindset

Fundraising is not easy. In fact, it is one of the most frustrating and time-draining activities you, as a founder, will have to undertake as part of your company's growth strategy. Early on, when you are just a small team, fundraising efforts will likely consume far more time than you'd like them to. Unfortunately, there is no shortcut to the process.

Unless you are really lucky and investors come to you, fundraising will likely involve taking many meetings with investors of all kinds, good and bad, before you ultimately succeed in finding someone who believes in you. Expect to meet many types of investors along the way including those who:

- Doubt you as a founder/CEO and your ability to execute.
- Meet with you because they want to invest in your competitor.
- Don't have the money to invest but want to appear active in the ecosystem (never hesitate to ask other founders for references on people you will reach out to!).
- Want every inch of detail about what you will be doing for the next five years, when you both know your projections will be speculative at best and hogwash at worst.
- Don't get what you do at all but will have an opinion about your product because their child, spouse, or close friend has a view.
- Are amazing and give you insanely poignant advice, but want to see more traction before they can consider investing.
- Provide you with great feedback and would help you greatly if they were involved, but will only invest if someone else leads the round.

And then there is the one investor who ultimately believes in you and backs you. That's all it takes. **Just one.**

The earlier the stage your company is in, the more fundraising is about your ability to develop personal relationships and articulate your ambitions as a coherent story (a.k.a. storytelling, more on that in a later chapter).

In the early days, the two main drivers behind why an investor will be drawn to you are fear of missing out (FOMO) and/or your growth metrics. Even investors with a thesis in your space are subject to the emotions these two drivers generate.

As much as some investors will want to know your projected numbers (revenues, traction, etc.), the conversation will always come back to your inherent abilities and vision as a founder, since there's little else to go on. This is where your ability to weave and deliver a compelling narrative about your vision will increase the likelihood of generating FOMO. This narrative is, in effect, an extension and proxy for your mindset to overcoming adversity and building something of meaning.

Fundraising meetings in the early phases of company development are, therefore, about sizing each other up. Investors want to see how the founders think through their assumptions and if they can work together, and founders need to assess whether they think the investor will add value to their startup.

This dynamic of imperfect information early-on leads to an apt analogy frequently used to describe the fundraising process: *dating*. As funny as it may seem, there are more similarities than differences. In fundraising, as in dating...

- You have to be willing to put yourself out there to meet anyone in the first place.
- It's a numbers game. You have to meet a lot of people,

either in person at networking events, parties or online.
- Rejections tend to hurt quite a bit, but you need to get over them fast.
- Connections usually happen in the least likely of places and are strongest when they come through a trusted third party
- Being a good storyteller gets people to laugh, open up, and remember you.
- Chemistry matters.
- Sometimes it's just plain luck—being at the right place at the right time.
- The better you prepare yourself, the better your odds get.
- Being too eager to get back to someone or waiting too long can end things prematurely.
- You have to go on several dates with multiple people before you ultimately feel someone is the right one for you.

Case in point: one of our founders (let's call him Tony), who I have the pleasure of working with to this day, was rejected 88 times before finally getting a yes from an investor. Reasons for the 'no's ranged from the usual "This won't ever be a big thing," to "There's someone already doing this." When Tony had one month's worth of cash left in his account, he took a flight and expensive car ride to another country to meet with an investor who, upon his arrival, admitted to having entirely forgotten about their meeting. The investor invited Tony to ride with him to his next meeting, and it was during this thirty-minute car ride that Tony finally got his yes.

Developing a fundraising mindset centers on four core ideas:

1. **Plan ahead.** Fundraising is a process that can take time

and is rarely quick or painless (with the exception of a select few). The earlier you start planning your process and developing relationships, the better off you will be, and the more likely you will be to avoid fundraising in "desperation mode."
2. **Expect rejection.** You have to embrace rejection as part of the process and not take it personally. Rejection will happen— for good reasons, dumb reasons and, many times, for reasons that will forever remain a mystery.
3. **Practice makes perfect.** Every meeting is a form of practice that makes you better for the next meeting. The success or failure of one meeting is never the end of your story, just a step along the way.
4. **Learn from the past.** Analyzing what was said during your meetings and learning how to improve on your mistakes is the most crucial step in finding the right investor more quickly. Just like you analyze your company's metrics, keep track of how people connected with your pitch; write down all the questions you were asked (a very good way of ascertaining which areas of your pitch are still ambiguous) and make sure you follow up on any information requests. Also, if you do get asked several types of questions repeatedly, consider incorporating the answers into your presentation or adding them to your appendix.

Since you will likely never know where, when or how you will meet your future investor, make sure you are always on the lookout for opportunities to develop relationships and possible connections for your company. Opportunities sometimes come from the most random encounters. In another story of unexpected outcomes, a founder was discussing some elements of her business with a colleague while riding on the London Tube. The person next to them identified himself as an investor and said, "Pitch me in one stop, and if it's good, I'll give you my contact details." The founder got a follow-up meeting out of the exchange. You just never know.

Timing Matters

Since fundraising intrinsically is a process of building the right relationships, and good-quality relationships take time to develop, don't leave fundraising to the last minute. The time from when you start taking meetings until close and cash-in-hand can take up to six months for an early-stage round. It can take an equal amount of time for subsequent rounds. Naturally, depending on how "frothy" or "exciting" the market you live in is and how experienced you are at fundraising, these timelines will vary.

Keeping your company financed isn't something you should procrastinate on. If you wait until you've nearly run out of cash you'll be in "desperation mode," making the process considerably more stressful and difficult.

Even if you aren't at risk of running out of capital, not thinking through when, how, and from whom you want to raise funds in the future risks you becoming a victim of circumstances, rather than being in control of them —or at least having a good plan on how to tackle them.

Don't defer planning or kicking off your fundraising process because you are waiting to finalize what you feel is going to be your product's killer feature either. Your idea is of no use to you or your team if you run out of money before making it a reality. As you'll read in the later chapters on milestones, there is a way to address the fear of not having your product at the level you want it to be when speaking to investors.

Over the last few years, two things have become apparent:

The first is how easily industry trends can come and go. Remember the Token/ICO craze of 2017, and then the Crypto/NFT craze of 2021 and subsequent crashes? Well, there are many sectors that go through similar, but less pronounced, swings. Yes, there is always the possibility that they can come back, but the more informed you are about where your company's industry is relative to these cycles, the better prepared you will be to tell a compelling narrative about why you aren't subject to either the wave of excitement (why you will survive) or the trough of despair (why now is the right time to invest).

The second is the power of relationships in getting things done. While I've already made the point that it takes time to build relationships, their power in the startup industry never ceases to amaze me. I think the days when you could just build a product without ever connecting with the larger community are long gone. Now, it is critical both for fundraising and, increasingly more importantly, for hiring key talent!

Geography Matters

One final point to touch upon before moving onto the fundraising process itself is that geography matters when raising funds.

As much as we'd all like there to be 100 percent mobility of capital globally, there isn't. There are plenty of amazing ideas and perfectly capable founders around the world; however, the bulk of the world's venture and angel capital is still very much aggregated around key hubs such as California, New York, Boston, London, Berlin, Paris, Israel and a select few others in Asia.

You will have different fundraising challenges depending on the mix of individual and institutional investors available in your home country and/or where you choose to raise. In a country where the funding comes mostly from individuals (such as professional angel investors and high-net-worth individuals), you will likely not be able to raise substantially large rounds; in countries where you have access to organized groups of individuals, you'll have access to larger rounds; and in countries where you have access to many institutional investors, you will likely be able to raise the largest rounds.

Suppose you want to go for really, really big sums (or target specific investors). In that case, you should go to the geography where you can get such meaningful amounts (otherwise you might under fund your company for what you need to achieve). But keep in mind that changing locales isn't as easy as packing up your bags and moving. In key financing hubs, the costs of running startups are going to be higher, so you will need to factor that into your plan. Issues that will increase your costs include immigration challenges (and lawyers), hiring star development talent, and office real estate. Remote working has made it possible to get the best of all worlds in some ways but, remote-first companies come with their own challenges and increasingly, some investors are having more in-depth chats with founders before investing to see whether they will be held hostage by the downsides of remote work (fractured team culture for one).

Regardless of where you raise, with each year that passes, it's amazing to see how quickly investment capital is being made available to more and more founders globally because of the maturation of venture capital as an investment asset class and because the cost to meet teams globally has declined due to the increase in using Zoom/Meets/Teams since Covid. Still, the fact remains that if you are based in an emerging economy, you'll have to work harder to connect with global sources of capital. Don't let this deter you from building something meaningful though. It is the job of capital to seek out amazing ideas—just make sure yours is one worth finding, and that you and your team are ready when the opportunity presents itself. Which reminds me...

An old parable tells of a man who was traveling. He came upon a farmer working in his field and asked him what the people in the next village were like. The farmer asked, "What were the people like in the last village you visited?" The man responded, "They were kind, friendly, generous, great people." "You'll find the people in the next village are the same," said the farmer.

Later, another man traveling to the same village approached the same farmer and asked what the people in the next village were like. Again the farmer asked, "What were the people like in the last village you visited?" The second man responded, "They were rude, unfriendly, dishonest people." "You'll find the people in the next village are the same," said the farmer.

No matter where in the world you choose to raise from, you and your mindset are ultimately the key variable that determines your outcomes.

2

Preparing Your Company for Fundraising

Setting the Right Milestones

Even though your company's journey will be a series of expected and unexpected events (hopefully more good than bad) over time, investors will typically want to hear your "projections" as a coherent linear strategy (the old expression goes *"Investors invest in lines, not dots"*, dots being data points, and lines being the trend between them). Better investors know that early-stage startups are fraught with uncertainty and thus will only use your stated strategy as starting and discussion points to test your thinking. Sadly, in contrast, investors/angels that come from careers in other areas of financing, such as debt or real estate, will likely give more weight to your linear strategy than it deserves early on.

Therefore, for your initial round of financing, the first step in communicating your fundraising needs to an investor is to determine a projection of your future cash requirements, typically for the next 12-18 months. The easiest way to do this is by visualizing your company's cash spend as a series of projected milestones. While I break down the concept of milestones below, I just want to clarify that how you communicate the total sum you are raising is different from how you got to that amount (see the format below). As with a first date, there is such a thing as TMI (too much information) when sharing with investors.

Determining projected milestones for your company will help you decide your financing needs and start a conversation with co-founders. You will need to figure out what should happen when, and how you should best use your resources. To be precise, **I define a milestone as a future "marker" or quantifiable achievement within your company's stated growth trajectory**, not just a major accomplishment at some vague, future time. Essentially, you can think of a milestone as a singular point on the company's projected timeline. Milestones usually mark defining points in a company's history, such as a key hire, a product launch, a certain number of users, a retention rate, first revenues, first profits, and so on.

Unlike the typical financial goal of any startup (i.e., the creation of a successful, cash-self-sufficient company that provides tangible value to its customers and is ultimately floated on the public market), milestones are specific events—subsets of that goal.

Defining milestones is important for various reasons. Knowing where milestones exist in your company's future can better prepare you for future fundraising. Fundraising at the tail end of (or right before) a meaningful milestone will put you on a stronger footing when in discussions with potential investors.

For example, let's look at the following milestones during a fictitious company's first year. You should not assume these are good time markers. *This timeline is purely for illustration purposes and isn't intended to showcase typical speed of growth or development.*

Month 1: Close a round with a well known pre-seed fund

Month 3: Launch of Alpha version of product or MVP (Minimum Viable Product)

Month 5: Launch Private Beta to a larger group of users

Month 8: A key person hire (eg. a marketing person from hyper-relevant company)

Month 11: Public Product Launch

Month 12: Achieve [X] percent daily growth rate in subscribers

Month 18: Raise the next round of financing

If you know how much money is needed, in aggregate, at each point in the timeline, you'll also know how much you need to raise to achieve each target. Additionally, once you have your milestones, you can evaluate which milestone speaks to individual investors most and where you could spend more money to go faster if need-be (or save money, if needed). Different investors have different views on what determines "progress" in a startup. For example, a functional prototype can be a hugely validating achievement for an early-stage investor even if there aren't any customers yet. As such, *some of the best times for a company to fundraise are either right before or right after the completion of a key milestone*, but before so much time passes that the recently achieved milestone is no longer impressive.

To understand why the above is the case, the challenge to an early-stage investor is to balance investing in your startup before you are too far along in your progress (and thus merit a higher valuation) and coming in too early in your journey (and risk losing it all). All investors strive to minimize risk without losing the opportunity to invest in a hot company, for the earlier they invest, the higher the likelihood of achieving greater returns. Investors are constantly trying to find the least risky point at which to invest so as to avoid the risk of losing their entire investment, which is not a-typical at pre-seed and seed stages.

Fundraising Before a Key Milestone

First, let's look at the psychology of investing right before a key milestone is completed.

Suppose an investor feels confident that the company is on

track to hit a milestone. They also know that once it succeeds, the company will inherently be more valuable to the outside market because it has been de-risked by some meaningful amount. As such, the investor wants to get in on the deal right before "launch", so that they can get a "better deal" valuation-wise (or get "access") while the company is still a little bit riskier, but not overly so.

While this makes obvious sense, only companies that instill strong confidence and FOMO in potential investors regarding the company's growth or value post-milestone-completion can get investors rushing to get this kind of deal done.

If you can make this happen for your company, you're in a great position, because generally, a product-launch milestone is easier for you to control than, say, a specific user growth rate after your product's launch.

Fundraising After a Key Milestone

Now let's look at the psychology of investing after a key milestone is completed.

Suppose an investor seems like she wants to stall —to see if the milestone is completed or the number of users you acquire hits a specified figure— then she is trying to effectively de-risk the investment before committing cash. An investor knows that by playing their cards this way, not only will they have de-risked the investment somewhat, but other investors will also be more likely to co-fund your company alongside them. In effect, the post-milestone investor wants to get in quickly before the company is too expensive an investment for her, but is only willing to move when the "right level" of de-risking has occurred. This behavior isn't just limited to the early stages of a company's financing history—I've seen this behavior across the lifecycle of all startups!

The art of selecting the right moment for fundraising is a matter of determining which key milestones to focus on and how to communicate them during your meetings with potential investors.

Let's look more closely at four key types of milestones. Within these four categories are a fair number of potential additional milestones. Which milestones are most meaningful to your company and potential investors is up to you to determine.

The Four Types of Milestones

1. Human resources

A first milestone could be hiring key people who will make a strong impact on your organization (a super-relevant marketing person, for example). If your team is a power team already, milestones could include proof that you can attract additional talent and work well together as a team (usually historical evidence, such as having worked together in the past, helps). Key hires are C- and VP-level professionals who will drive your growth further. Every startup will eventually need a functioning management team consisting of a CEO, CTO, COO, VP of Sales, VP of Marketing, and possibly some others, depending on what you're building and stage.

2. Product: launches vs. incremental version releases

A milestone here could be proof that you can build something (i.e. a working prototype), or the launch of a major enabler for a step-change in customer acquisition. Note that there is a difference between milestones that you might articulate to an company reaches and when. Be sure your fundraising strategy uses these milestones to your benefit without getting caught between them, stranded for cash.

As a general rule, you should try to raise as much money as you can (within reason and which I'll explain in a later chapter) and in any case, at least enough money to accomplish your next meaningful milestone (with some additional buffer funds to help you spend time fundraising after the milestone and to avoid "desperation mode"). This means you should look at a variety of points across your company's timeline to see which will be meaningful milestones for fundraising purposes.

Identifying milestones for your company's development has myriad benefits besides those associated with fundraising. First, establishing milestones allows you to focus on what you will be working on and drive hard to achieve it. Second, the process of identifying and setting milestones forces you to question when and in what order you and your team should try to execute something. Lastly, having your milestones specified is useful for tying together what you need to accomplish with **how much money it will take to get there**, and thus fundraise accordingly.

Keeping Milestone Optionality

During your milestone definition exercise with your co-founders, consider doing what I call "keeping milestone optionality". We all know that in the early stages of a company, there is no such thing as a clear and linear path to success.

Thus, the milestone optionality principle is very simple: even as you plan your company's future growth and associated cash investor (say, a major release with key functionality) and those on your product roadmap (say, a "point" release that does an important, but less visibly impactful thing). Don't confuse the two, because they aren't the same thing.

3. Traction: market validation (first customers, first paying customers, etc.)

Here, you prove that you have access to your target audience (100,000, 1 million or 10 million users), that the product or service is useful to someone (first users and clients), or that there is a market ($1 million revenue annually). The proof may also be that you can scale ($10 million in revenue annually) or that the market and, therefore, future traction is big ($25 million in revenue annually and beyond)!

For a good starting place on how various metrics qualify you for different rounds (as a SaaS business) check out the "SaaS Funding Napkin" by Christoph Janz on the web. Christoph and the P9 team update it yearly.

4. Funding: money being committed to a round that the investor in question can lead or participate in

Milestones may include proof that you can talk to investors (every financing round, even small ones), proof that the ecosystem agrees with your ideas (bringing respected industry advisors or partnerships on board), or proof that you can manage your finances (cash flow positive operation). But a word of caution: as my friend and colleague Will Bennett reminded me, many great companies don't hit this consensus milestone until much later, so don't hold your breath waiting for everyone to validate you even if a few do!

Just keep in mind that milestones are all about moving from one stage of risk to the next. Plan your fundraising strategy to ensure you have ample time to control which milestones your needs, you can't lose sight of the fact that you're a nimble startup—not a large corporation that has to report to analysts and public market shareholders. Your nimbleness is your strength. As mentioned earlier, a startup's growth plan isn't linear (even if you sometimes need to communicate it that way); it's more like a series of zig zags toward a goal. Because of this, while it is important to forecast your milestones so that you have a plan and understand your cash needs, it is also useful to look at that plan with one eye, while the other eye looks out for actions that might be more beneficial to your company than what you had originally envisaged or agreed to with existing shareholders.

You may have heard of tranched investments, which release funds in parts based on predetermined conditions (or milestones). In a later chapter, we will discuss in more detail why you should try to avoid tranched investments but, their popularity does come and go depending on the times, so let's briefly cover why here.

If you consider a tranche as glorified milestone, adhering dogmatically to it early on could have a negative impact. Why? Well, because endeavoring to meet the scheduled conditions may constrain your company's growth options, especially if midway through executing your stated strategy it turns out the goal agreed upon for the tranche release was a bad idea for the company.

For example, imagine if your financial plan had a monetization strategy (and associated revenue stream) in place, kicking off in "Month Six" of your operations. "Month Six" comes along and, well, uptake is poor and your revenues are not coming in as expected. Additionally, you have some chats with your customers and find out that actually, the value they're getting from your product is mostly around its emerging network effect. Yet, because the network is still small, your early monetization plan is stifling that value since the barrier for new users to sign up is still high, and thus those most likely to pay are reluctant to do so.

If you (or your investors) adhere rigidly to your original plan just for the sake of keeping to it to get the next tranche, you could quickly kill your company's potential long-term value. But by staying nimble and adapting your milestones to what you believe should be the new direction, your company could be better off.

Naturally, optionality comes at a cost, but that's okay as long as you fully understand how things are changing. A goal shift means your original plan changes, so other goals change, your cash burn will change, and the key performance indicators (KPIs)— markers that show your company's success and typically the markers for some tranches—will also change.

Good early-stage investors (particularly those who invest in pre-product-market fit companies) know that this kind of change midway through their funding is possible and should back you in your ability to make these difficult calls, even if it means a deviation from the original plan. However, be mindful that there are many investors out there who, for some reason, still believe firmly in adherence to a stated plan (likely because in other industries, CEOs are held accountable far more for this). If you can, avoid taking money from these kinds of investors. At the very early stages in a company's development, particularly during the pre-product-market fit phase, backers should invest in you for your ability to adapt to changing and evolving circumstances, not in your ability to predict the future eighteen months in advance or stick to a plan that clearly isn't working.

Although you should constantly be on the lookout for milestone optionality plays coming up, this isn't a recommendation to throw out all forms of planning. it still helps to create a milestone plan based on your hypothesis of growth (and relevant KPIs) and cash needs, because of course you can't be changing strategies every month and you need to keep an eye on cash burn. If you do find, however, that you are constantly questioning your original growth hypothesis, perhaps there is a bigger problem you are facing (such as the need for better internal processes). By keeping an eye open for milestone optionality events, you might fare better than you would if you exercised uber-discipline to a rigid plan built before you learned many new things about your customers and how they interact with your product.

As a general rule, plan for the future and identify key milestones to grow towards, but seek to keep milestone optionality, particularly at a pre-product-market fit stage.

How Much Money Should I Raise?

As mentioned earlier, raising money for your startup takes time, distracts you from developing your product, is fraught with emotional ups and downs, and unfortunately doesn't have a guaranteed outcome to compensate for these negatives. Frankly, many founders would rather jump into an icy lake than take another fundraising meeting where they aren't sure what they should say to "convince" an already-hesitant investor to open their purse strings.

Part of that anxiety comes from not knowing what, exactly, investors have in mind when evaluating the company, particularly when it comes to cash needs.

So naturally, the question becomes: how much money should I raise?

The short version of the answer is "as much as you can." But just to cover all bases, let's look at the extremes. When is "raising as much as you can" potentially harmful?

While raising as much money as possible all at once sounds great, you can't operate under the assumption that more money early on means fewer problems to worry about.

Too Much

A large amount of money early on comes with several potential problems. I cover this in more detail in the next chapter, but just to lay the groundwork, below are four downsides to raising too much capital:

1. **More investment terms and more due diligence**. It is probably fair to say that the more money involved, the more investment provisions an investor will want, as well as more "process" to ensure their money isn't misused.
2. **A "high" implied** post-money valuation[1] or, alternatively, higher dilution up front. To accommodate a large round, investors need to adjust your valuation accordingly if they don't want to wash you and your founders out. For example, if your business is objectively worth $5 million (we'll cover valuations in a separate chapter), but you are raising $10 million, unless the investor plans on owning 66 percent of the company after investment, the valuation

---

[1] http://en.wikipedia.org/wiki/Post-money_valuation

will have to be adjusted upward. Having an artificially higher valuation prematurely to avoid too much dilution (and still raise a large round) can put a lot of strain on your startup. If things don't go well and another round of fundraising is needed later on, either it will likely be a down-round (when your valuation takes a negative hit), or other new investors will pass on the deal in the future because it is "too expensive."

3. **The propensity to misuse "easy money"**. You could argue this point from a psychological perspective if you wanted to, but suffice it to say, I know many VCs who believe overfunding a company leads to financial laxity, lack of focus, and overspending by the management team. Perhaps it is a lingering fear from the heydays of previous boom-and-bust cycles when parties were rampant and everyone got fancy, over-priced perks. However, the general fear about overfunding a company is that its founders will be tempted to expand faster than they can absorb employees into the culture, integrate new systems, or meet real-estate needs without substantially disrupting efficient operations.

4. **The media's reaction (positive or negative) to how much money you've raised** relative to what you have achieved. This one is hard to really quantify and happens to only a few startups. For example, in 2012, a serial entrepreneur raised $41 million out of the starting blocks for a company called Color. Even by 2023 standards, this is a large number! Unfortunately, the app went nowhere and didn't satisfy the promise expected of it for that kind of money, making it, at the time, the source of many jokes about the perils of raising too much money early on (Color

eventually shut down a year after its re-launch). Although clearly a rare case, it demonstrates what the "too much" effect can cause. In 2015, the case of the startup called Secret shutting down after raising $35 million, which the founders cashed out a portion of, also left investors with a bad taste. For another case study, look up the story of Quibi, a short-form video streaming platform that raised $1.75 billion from investors and shut down in under a year with little to show for it. Finally, more recently, during the post-covid boom, several NFT companies raised tons of cash and have since imploded for various reasons (FTX, for example).

On the subject of raising too much capital, my colleague Tom Wilson and fellow friend Check Warner penned a great article on The Danger of Venture Capital Foie Gras on https://sifted.eu/ check it out! Lastly, if you really want to go down a rabbit hole, check out "463 startup failure post-mortems" by CBInsights for a list of over 400 companies that have failed over time and why (and not just funding-related).

Too Little

Moving from too much to too little: underfunding your company. One of the risks you run when being willing to take a cash amount you know is insufficient for you to achieve any one of your meaningful milestones is that you will likely not be able to demonstrate any substantial progress before you need to go out fundraising again. As a result, you will raise in "desperation mode" or "drip-feed mode." While there are exceptions (you're first starting out and just trying to validate the hypothesis or bridging your company's fundraising by raising a little cash to get you to the next major milestone), avoid raising too little money. It will very likely put you in a weak fundraising position as you'll have to fundraise again too soon (which is a bad use of time) and may look bad to investors tracking your progress vis-a-vis your competitors and goals you stated the last time you spoke to them.

"Okay, I get it—too much or too little money can be bad. So how much money is the right amount of money?"

Let's look at this question from a different point of view. As we will cover later on during the section on how an investor evaluates your financial plan, an investor may not necessarily know the exact figures your business will need to grow to its next major milestone. Instead, to some extent, an investor will rely on your ability to communicate your financial plan and review your cash needs relative to your stated goals.

Know Your Cash Burn

Monthly cash burn, or the total amount of money you "burn" through each month, is a key figure to know before meeting any investor. You're in trouble if you don't know your expected monthly cash burn based on your fundraising hopes. Without it, you are likely to struggle to have a good dialogue with investors about cash needs and representative accomplishments needed to demonstrate traction. Thus, it should start to become apparent, as we discuss this further, why it is so important for you to have a solid understanding of your cash needs for hiring, customer acquisition and overall company growth. Your cash-use hypotheses will become the foundations for your discussions with investors.

So, alongside the timeline of milestones you and your co-founders will establish, you'll need to develop a parallel schedule of cash milestones. The "cash milestone timeline" represents how much money, in aggregate, you will have spent to achieve each milestone you set out to accomplish in your strategic plan e.g. cash needs to drive growth plans, make key hires or acquire new customers.

Referring back to my examples of milestones in a company's first year, we might find a cash timeline that looks something like this (*I've purposely put in fictitious numbers; do not assume these are recommendations or actual numbers as if we fast forward 20 years into the future, I bet that due to inflation, we'll have to add a zero to each of these!*):

Month 6 - $60,000
  Month 8 - $80,000
  Month 10 - $100,000
  Month 11 - $110,000
  Month 12 - $120,000
  Month 18 - $240,000

Here I've used a $10,000 monthly cash burn up to the end of Year 1. Then, starting in Year 2, a $20,000 monthly cash burn. Thinking this part through is critical. If you raise less money than necessary to reach a major milestone, you'll likely fall short of cash before your company has anything substantial to impress investors with.

Know How to Frame the Conversation

Let's assume you've now calculated your ideal cash needs and the amount seems a bit higher than what your local investors are willing to offer. You're likely asking yourself the following questions:

- If I ask for the amount I truly need, but that is above what investors are willing to give, doesn't it automatically set me up for a no and then later having to backtrack?
- If I ask for a smaller amount, won't investors know I need more money than I'm asking for?
- If I ask for too little, will I sound like I don't know what I'm doing?
- What's the best way to kick off a conversation with an investor in a non-hub/non-core-VC market to get across my desire to raise more capital if available, but my willingness to take less cash and make the best of it if not?
- How do I avoid getting pigeon-holed into not being a big enough thinker or having priced myself out of the local market?

This is where understanding your milestones and cash timeline comes in handy as it allows you to know the impact of all these trade-offs on what you can achieve. The quick, blunt and rather unsatisfying answer to the above questions is "It's a two-way conversation with the investor." It's as much about you interviewing them as them you.

These conversations are never easy. So the longer answer is: you need to really invest time in pre-qualifying whom you talk to, understand whether they can "afford" to invest (or not) in your round, and make sure you know how to address the key concerns they may have for the stage of risk they perceive you are in. One thing you should never do is compromise on your "vision" for the company.

In some geographies, you can be as ambitious as you want and sometimes that's not enough. Within these geographies (e.g., the Valley and London, to name a couple), you need to be able to tell a story that gets your company to Billion Dollar ambitions to really excite key funds. Without that kind of vision, many large funds will just not think it is a big enough idea to really inspire their commitment as their fund size requires startup exit sizes big enough to return the funds and that's hard to do on ideas where the exit scenarios are smaller.

However, in other geographies, unfortunately, local investors can be quite negative about more overly ambitious fundraises and sometimes operate on a very near-term cash basis. This is because many a smaller investor has been burned by promises and hopes that go nowhere. Since the writing of this book's original version, unfortunately this more fearful approach this still exists. Luckily, however, it is quickly changing as more and more successful founders become angels themselves.

One way of tackling the fundraising conversation when speaking with an investor who is notoriously keen on "short-term plausible accomplishments" and put off by "unrealistic big statements" is to articulate your round in a way where you don't compromise on your vision, but appeal to their shorter-term thinking. For example:

"I want my company to accomplish 'X' over the next few years, but

in the near term, I believe we can get to 'Y' and in order to do so, we are raising 'Z'."

By framing the cash request conversation this way, you've opened up the conversation about what cash generates what outcome and avoided sounding like you're asking for too much too early vis-a-vis this fictitious investor's risk profile. Furthermore, by framing the conversation on what you achieve and when, you will have demonstrated you understand that you need to achieve things before you can likely go fundraising again. In effect, you're trying to articulate confidence to an investor based on your knowledge of what it will take for you to be successful.

However, as I stated, **never compromise on your long-term vision.** It's just that at times, you'll have to fight to survive. But hey —you were expecting that anyway!

Investors: Who's Who and How Much Can Each Provide?

Investors come in different sizes and styles. The most obvious ones are friends and family, but shortly after them come business angels, or high-net-worth individuals who are willing to invest in your startup in exchange for equity. There are many variants of angels. Some are just simply investing out of their own pockets. Others can be aggregations of business angels—angel clubs—or syndicates like those possible online via crowd-funding platforms such as AngelList, Seedrs, Crowdcube, etc. (which we cover in the Appendix).

An angel investor who invests their own money typically invests in the tens or hundreds of thousands of Dollars, but less so in the millions (particularly if you're not living in a major hub of angel investing; in the US, however, these sums can go up). As opposed to your friends and family, angels will typically want to see more progress in your company before committing to an investment. They will likely want to come in early enough to give you cash so you can achieve something, plus a little extra to help you fundraise afterward (so they can get more equity for their capital than they would if they came in later). However, these angels may also hold back some additional cash for a follow-on round, so that they can commit further when they see you can achieve your milestones. While this is not unusual, it is different from a tranched investment (more on this in a later segment of this book), where typically a larger amount of cash is committed upfront with specific conditions and at greater dilution to you.

Continuing from the previous example earlier in this book, an angel (or angels) may opt to fund your cash needs of $100,000 through Month 10, plus a little extra for more fundraising —perhaps an additional $50,000— for a total of maybe $150,000-300,000 (as of 2023, this figure can be multiplied by 2-3x due to round inflation since the second version of this book). This would get you through your product launch and give you a couple of months to see how it goes in terms of market traction so you can have something stronger to discuss for fundraising purposes. (Though, all the while, you will be speaking to new potential investors.)

Moving on from angels, institutional investors invest other people's and their own money (via their fund). For example, a seed-stage venture capital fund—a type of institutional investor—may see that your company has some real potential and that your plan requires $150,000-1,500,000 to launch before you start trying to monetize. But, the seed fund's partners might think — based on their experience of seeing your kind of business having to do a few pivots before getting the launch product 100 percent right— that perhaps the best quantity to give you based on your calculations is $2,000,000-3,000,000 for about a year to a year and a half. This larger amount would also give you some breathing room to work on achieving your various milestones rather than constantly having to be in fundraising mode.

Considering the two examples above, why is it that two types of investors can have different perceptions of how much money you need? Well, the sad reality is that each investor sees the world through their own eyes. The smaller investor sees smaller rounds and the larger investor larger rounds (to a reasonable limit, as naturally there is a point when it becomes silly and they'd just rather pass).

With these differing views, how can you determine how much money an investor actually thinks you need vis-a-vis what you ask for?

Round Size Implications

This ambiguity about fundraising quanta is both your friend and a source of frustration. Your exact calculations may have indicated that you needed $500,000 to launch your product. Yet, an experienced investor might know that for companies such as yours, there are usually issues along the way that consume cash without the requisite quantifiable progress toward the agreed milestones. Because of this, investors may sometimes include "cash buffers" in the number they offer you in a deal, even if they don't articulate it that way (think for example of businesses with regulatory or inventory needs). This buffer could come from the various sensitivity analyses the investor evaluates.

For example, what if a company is delayed in launching their product by two months, can't find that key employee, or can't start charging for their product for an extra few months? Or what if the product needs a pivot, or people aren't willing to pay what the company expected? All of these things will affect the company's cash flow. If the investor assumes some or all will occur, they will realize that the company may need more money than the founder planned for. Effectively, your $500,000 in a perfect milestone execution timeline may actually end up being more like $2 million after some delays and mistakes. With the extra cash the institutional investor in my example gave you, you may now have enough cash to go fundraise your next round without having to panic about getting cash in yesterday. Once again, you're avoiding "desperation mode"—one of your major goals during the fundraising process.

Keep in mind that the larger amount an investor may be willing to give you will affect your company's valuation range. Valuation is closely linked to the amount of money you raise through a simple equation:

Money raised/post-money valuation of the round = percentage dilution of the round.

Solving for a fixed-percentage dilution expectation, too much money upfront will "inflate" the valuation range your company sits in (unless the investor is willing to take more equity), so an investor won't want to give you an excessive cash buffer that would force the company to be overpriced both for them and for the company's fundraising future. Inversely, you can also see where an investor may deem a company "underfunded" if it doesn't have enough money to get to where it can achieve meaningful milestones and attract future investors.

Different investors will come up with different numbers for your company's ideal fundraising strategy based on their experience and what they can offer. With this knowledge, be open to the wisdom gained from multiple perspectives.

If you meet an investor who wants to invest a lot quickly, great. If you meet with various investors who are more risk-averse, at least you won't get caught not understanding your own execution plan. As a general rule of thumb, many early-stage VCs will consider your cash needs over a twelve-to-eighteen-month period based on the averages they see in their geographies when trying to determine what you should raise before you need to go fundraising again.

In conclusion, the most important thing is to be keenly aware of your month-to-month cash needs, so if the question comes up during a discussion with an investor, you know how much you plan to spend and by when. In the end, embracing the ambiguity and fluidity of this process is the best way to avoid frustration with the contrasting conversations you will likely have with investors. As long as you know your monthly cash burn across various milestones and/or when you will run out of money, you'll be armed with the knowledge you need to have meaningful conversations with them.

3

Round Sizing: Further Implications

More is always better right? Or is it?

As I mentioned in the previous chapter, one of the interesting phenomena that developed as part of the Covid and post-Covid period was the explosion of round sizes and high valuations.

The reasons for this explosion were due to both startups and investors. There was startups' desire to::

1 - Reduce the need to raise again any time soon (time management)

2 - Showcase their company's success over competitors' with the amount of funds raised (company brand signaling / ego)

3 - Minimize dilution relative to funds raised (fear and 'being protective')

4 - Maximize funds available to hire talent faster than others (competitive dynamics)

Then there were investors who, in a desperate attempt to win rounds, competed against each other by signaling to founders that they should take more money which, of course, happened to be theirs (as we saw in the fundraising equation, a larger raise implies a larger valuation, which seems like it's lower dilution to founders, but which then forces a larger appetite for a larger return and higher difficulty of fundraising if you don't perform).

With all the easy money that was available, many founders were able to raise rounds that were in excess of what was likely needed. The result was a cascade of challenges that many companies are still trying to overcome.

Sure, there are benefits to raising a lot of money—if you are someone that can leverage that money effectively, you can dominate your competition/segment, hire the best talent (because you can afford to pay over the market and take them from your competitors), and perhaps move faster on tech development. However, these are not all givens. In order to do them, you need to raise a meaningful amount of money, not just a few million dollars above the average ask, and you need to do it from top investors or it can create the wrong outcome with unfortunate consequences.

These consequences include, in varying degrees, the following:

1 - Post-money valuations after a large round can leave many companies stranded on a 'high ledge'. Without enough meaningful progress before needing to raise again, companies face many investors 'passing on investing' simply due to the price needed to keep the company at it's previous high valuation, and few companies 'grow into a high valuation'.

2 - Employees, aware of the sums of money raised, expect

larger salaries (vs the typical wealth-creating equity grants), breaking the typical faith-driven attitude to joining an early stage company, whose culture is forged, not purchased.

3 - Perceptions of "speed to execute" are warped by much longer cash runways. Many companies lose the sense of urgency that is necessary to really maximize outcomes in a highly competitive market by having much more capital available.

4 - Polarization of the shareholder base between those who are passengers in the company's destiny because of their relatively small contribution (angel investors, friends and family) and those who are really holding the company's future in their hands. This may manifest very starkly when larger investors, often VCs, don't bail out the company with leading a bridge-loan when the company needs help due to their relatively larger contribution to the round.

5 - Lack of Focus is something that can also manifest with excess capital, as you can 'technically' afford many more projects which can distract you from keeping the 'main thing' the 'main thing'. It also doesn't help that if you have lots of capital, just simply keeping it generating interest and/or foreign exchange swings can keep you occupied on excessive cash management vs generating value.

5 - Founders finding themselves at odds with future investors because a large war chest raises investor expectations about outcomes. In effect, this creates an environment where many shareholders will be hesitant to speak the blunt truth if things go south.

In response to these concerns, I guess you can always ask the question, "So what? Those days are over anyway. It's hard enough raising now post-bubble to worry about that."

Take them as a warning for future times when things may once again become warped. Let them remind you, as a founder, to reflect on one key weapon you have in the early stages of your company's development: the forging of your company's culture through the natural adversity that comes with creating something new with others who are with you because they believe in you and the cause over all else.

That is a huge weapon that needs to be harnessed and developed, for ultimately, it will become what defines your company.

4

The Fundraising Process

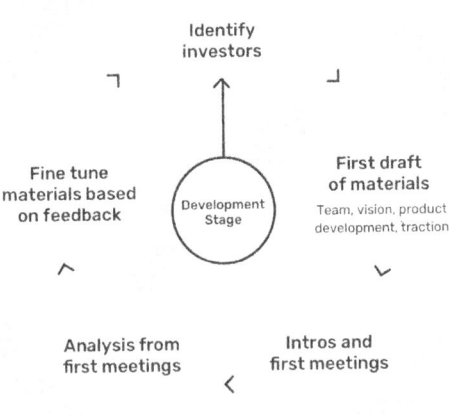

The Investment Materials Cycle

The Cycle of Fundraising

The fundraising process is highly iterative. It's almost impossible to understand what to say and how to say it for maximum positive effect without going through several fail cycles first. Assumptions that made sense to you and your team members are suddenly not as obvious to strangers who have never heard your idea before. Demos fail, jokes bomb, and people get distracted by materials you thought were crystal clear.

Thus, like the Taoist farmer whose story introduces this book, you have to view every interaction with investors as a learning opportunity by not judging any situation. There is no utility in coloring such experiences as "good" or "bad" as it'll likely just make you take the interactions too personally. Observe reactions and learn from your encounters with investors. Constantly fine-tune your materials, including your pitch, to achieve better results each time. As a caveat, "fine-tune" does not mean "cater to your audience". Stick to the core of what you believe your business is about, but learn to decouple what the core of your business is from how you present it. Many times, what other people reject isn't the idea itself, but how it is represented.

Additionally, it is important to keep an open mind when receiving rejections. Assess whether the rejection and its reasons make sense as you iterate and evolve your pitch. Remember that a person's mood—a factor over which you have very little or no control—might affect their interpretation of your pitch as much as the quality of the pitch itself. *Thinking, Fast and Slow* provides insight into how even things like hunger can negatively affect the outcome of a decision. In a study done in Israel on verdicts by judges, it turned out that when approaching meal-time, approval verdicts were close to zero, yet after meal times, approval rates would spike up to 65 percent! The study suggests a significant link between external—and often personal—conditions and decision-based outcomes. In other words, you can't control whether the investor has had lunch before or after your call, but there are ample things you can do to improve your chances in other ways.

Now that we have covered some of the key elements to consider to prepare your mindset for fundraising, let's look at what stops the fundraising cycle in its tracks. In other words, what should you NOT do when fundraising. Below is the top ten list of fundraising fails.

10. Presenting with a style that doesn't capture the right attention

Yes, being over-the-top and dropping f-bombs might get you attention, but is it the right kind? Are you focusing attention on your message, or just yourself? On the other hand, what about a boring slide deck? Or a deck that is missing product shots? Do these represent you well? What if you say your product is simple but then your deck is really over-complicated? Does that sound right?

9. Not having a proper fundraising plan

Fundraising requires research. Find out if your potential investors are even interested in your sector. Have they invested in your competitor? What amount do they typically invest? Going to someone who is typically a late-stage investor when you are raising a little bit of money is like ordering ten pizzas when you can only eat one.

8. Not understanding your customers or how to reach them

When presenting or speaking about your customers, do you

demonstrate a masterful grasp of their issues and identity? Do you understand what makes them tick and why your solution is the one that will likely best serve their needs? Do you also understand how to reach them? Where do they shop? What media do they consume?

7. Not demonstrating a real pain for your customers (and how your solution fixes it)

It's always tempting to create something useful for yourself. But, is the solution you've created really a necessity or just a nice-to-have? Demonstrating a real pain suffered by many, usually through some form of real customer validation, is crucial to making a convincing argument for your startup. Note that you should avoid asking someone an obvious question where the answer is yes but doesn't validate anything. If you aren't sure about how to ask the "right" questions to ascertain whether there is real customer pain, the best book on the subject is titled The Mom Test[2], by my friend Rob Fitzpatrick. I highly recommend it.

6. Assuming that a general market-size study applies to your startup

One of the things you can do to quickly show you don't have a full grasp of your market is to show a much larger segment than the one you operate in. For example, I've seen pitches where an iOS app for sports tracking mentions all mobile users worldwide as its market size, when in reality, its market is a sub-segment of that bigger pie. Understand the difference between your target/addressable market and the general market your company operates in.

5. Failing to understand who your competitors are

---

[2] http://momtestbook.com

This one is easy. Rarely are there ideas that no one has thought about before. If you think you don't have competitors, you probably haven't researched hard enough. And savvy investors might just know who they are, making you look bad if you don't know. But more importantly, sometimes there are "good enough" substitutes for your product that you need to be aware of. Show how your solution overcomes the momentum that those existing solutions already have and/or how an adjacent 'big-tech' can't just easily enter into this market.

4. Not knowing your cash needs and cash burn

If you're fundraising and you don't know how much money you need, how long it will take you to achieve what, and how you will spend the money you receive... well, don't fault investors if they aren't impressed with your request for investment.

3. Not explaining why your team is the team that will make it happen

Your team is 99 percent of why your company succeeds, and the idea is probably 1 percent. If you skim over the "why" of why your team is the right one for this investment, you'll likely miss an opportunity to impress an investor. Later in this book, how an investor reviews your team is covered, which will shed light on what angels and VCs are looking for.

2. Your existing investor shareholders own more equity than the founders

Toxic rounds unfairly skewed to a few shareholders (typically external investors) that preceded the current round you are raising for can dramatically affect your fundraising plan. In general, try to make sure you take investments that don't jeopardize your future ability to raise follow-on funds.

1. Not reaching out to an investor through an introduction

Lastly, the best thing you can do for yourself is secure a personal introduction to investors you want to meet. Introductions are great ways to show immediate validation and can overcome many of the above issues simply through the trusted relationship of whomever introduced you.

BONUS: Not learning from your mistakes

Learn from your mistakes. You will make many, and that's okay—as long as you don't beat yourself up. Understand what went wrong, find the correction, and then iterate on it. In the words of Albert Einstein, "Insanity is doing the same thing over and over and expecting different results."

Conventional wisdom maintains that if you had to boil down the role of a CEO into just two activities, they would be fundraising (communicating the vision to investors to get cash to keep the company going) and hiring (setting the culture and finding the right people to get stuff done).

Fundraising can easily become a cycle that companies start and never really get out of until they choose to stop (typically at an exit). So it helps to just put yourself into the frame of mind that you are always fundraising. Even right after closing a round, you should know who you will need to form relationships with for the next round.

In summary, the fundraising cycle involves:

- Creating your fundraising materials and networking both of which we will cover in more detail in later chapters
- Shopping around for investors and building relationships
- Receiving initial offers
- Choosing an offer(s) and negotiating
- Signing a term sheet when you feel confident about one of

your offers, then drafting and managing the legal process
- Closing and transfer of funds

When completed, simply rinse and repeat until you are either cash-flow positive and can finance growth internally or no longer need to finance for other reasons.

Now that we've looked at the basics of the start of the fundraising cycle, it's time to move on to the most important element in your fundraising efforts: the tools and materials that represent you and building the relationships that connect you.

5

Your Fundraising Materials

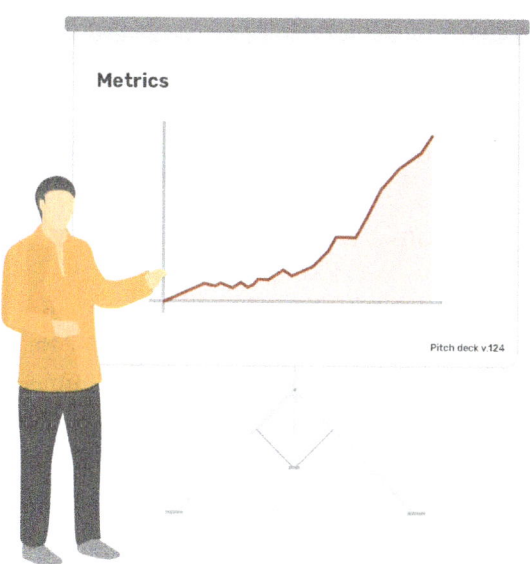

If you tell me, it's an essay. If you show me, it's a story.
  —Barbara Greene

I wanted a perfect ending. Now I've learned, the hard way, that some poems don't rhyme, and some stories don't have a clear beginning, middle, and end. Life is about not knowing, having to change, taking the moment and making the best of it, without knowing what's going to happen next. Delicious Ambiguity.
  —Gilda Radner

Why was Solomon recognized as the wisest man in the world? Because he knew more stories (proverbs) than anyone else. Scratch the surface in a typical boardroom and we're all just cavemen with briefcases, hungry for a wise person to tell us stories.
  —Alan Kay, Vice-President, The Walt Disney Company

The Backdrop from a Decade of Easy Money

The time period from 2010 to 2022 will go down in history as a time of overly-generous capital at low cost, for many companies globally. In particular, during and immediately following the COVID period, costs of capital were at record lows, leading to many kinds of unsustainable behaviors in public and private markets. Everyone started feeling invincible in different ways, whether it was in their ability to generate returns, sales, or fundraise. This led to a series of behaviors that would be unsustainable in non-close-to-zero-interest-rate environments.

  Because there were some easy wins during the previous

decade, I noticed the fragmentation of advice given to founders to capitalize on this capital availability. However, this advice was not tailored to the circumstances of each founding team. There were some founders giving advice on what worked for them to other founders who were not operating with the same variables as them, as if the same strategy should work over and over again in an ever-changing environment. As an example, I recently heard of a founder who advised another founder not to create any kind of fundraising materials so that they could feign being too busy with traction and inbound investor interest to have time to prepare them. This of course backfires quickly when investors get wind that it's all for show, and it's incredibly hard for investors to regain confidence in a founder once they know they were being played.

In other words, run your own race. It's great to get advice from others, but don't assume that the context that allowed them to raise money easily (or with lots of difficulty) will apply to you.

Keeping Materials Lean

Continuing from the above, and starting with the basics, to begin fundraising you will need simple communication materials. They don't need to be complex, they don't need to be excessive, but you do need something to tell your story. This includes the following materials:

- What others will use to introduce you to potential investors
- Those you send investors that show more details about your strategy, financially and execution-wise
- Something that shows the current equity structure between

founders.

As you will likely have many things to do as an early-stage founder, the best way to think of these materials is not as a burden, but as the leanest form of communication to benefit your company.

Luckily for you, though, the days of lengthy business plans are long gone (or should be anyway). Investors rarely have the time to read them anymore. Therefore, optimize your materials to be concise and address key issues to communicate your story, and no more.

However, this doesn't mean you shouldn't sweat the details, beginning even with your startup's name. In his book, Thinking, Fast and Slow[3], author Daniel Kahneman points to research that highlights the importance of not just what you name your company but how much detailed thinking you need to give many "trivial" aspects of your presentation. In his words: "A study conducted in Switzerland found that investors believe that stocks with fluent names like Emmi, Swissfirst, and Comet will earn higher returns than those with clunky labels like Geberit and Ypsomed." (An Axios story by Sara Fischer on " How to name your startup "has some great tips by Rich Barton.)

The moral of the story is that you must pay attention to the details, no matter how trivial they may seem. It all begins with your startup's name and investor materials, as they are the foundation of the crucial first impression you'll make on prospective investors.

---

[3] https://en.wikipedia.org/wiki/Thinking,_Fast_and_Slow

While there are many different opinions about what constitutes the ideal set of fundraising materials, the below list is a good start:

1. **Intro summary**. A paragraph or two summary of what your company is about. As basic as this sounds, you will likely be sending this very summary to your personal network for them to forward via messaging or email on your behalf for introductions.
2. The **pitch deck** you will use when presenting verbally. Naturally, you'll have to develop the verbal pitch that accompanies this deck.
3. **A pitch deck with more detail** based on #2 above, but that will make sense to an investor without your verbal presentation. This could be simply be the one above but with an appendix.
4. Your **financial assumptions model**, to showcase how you are thinking about cash use.
5. Your **cap table**, with the equity distribution between your team members.
6. Your **online profile** on AngelList, LinkedIn, X (formerly Twitter), and any other meaningful platforms that are typically used to learn more about your company.

For delivery of the above materials, besides sending them as a mere 'attachments' in an email, feel free to use Notion, Dropbox, and Docsend, which I'll cover in more detail later in this chapter.

Let's now explore each of these communication materials in more detail..

Your Intro Summary

When you go to the movies and see an epic trailer, you're naturally drawn to want to see the movie when it launches. Similarly, the purpose of your summary is to entice the recipient to want to learn more about what you're doing. Since an investor's attention is at a premium early on given the many deal options available to them, the Intro Summary should provide them with as much information as possible, with the least amount of effort on your part.

The Summary should be a work of art that represents you, your brand, your tone, and your personality. The reason why I say 'a work of art' is because, in the words of Mark Twain, (along with many to whom this quote is attributed) "If I had more time, I would have written a shorter letter". It is an art-form to be able to captivate a reader about what you are working on, why it is relevant and showcase any numerical data and momentum, all in a way that is easy to read and succinct.

This Summary will be your fundraising calling card. It is the 'blurb' that you will email to anyone who can forward it to others on your behalf. It is what you cut and paste onto messaging platforms. It is in effect, your first step in.

The Pitch Deck

As mentioned earlier, most investors that are good and in-demand don't have time to read anything more than the executive summary of what is sent to them. So should you even bother creating a pitch deck? What should one look like? And what might it say about you?

First, let's start by defining what a modern-day pitch deck could look like. I'd say, the idea is that after reading it, anyone should be able to clearly understand what your business is about without having to speak to you. For the deck you'll present verbally, you'll likely use the same version as the more detailed one, but with some text removed where the key points should be made verbally. Nowadays,, even the definition of a 'deck' is up for grabs as more and more founders are using Notion to have more of a 'web page' that presents all elements of their company. However, for the sake of simplicity, I'll refer to any long-form presentation of what you are doing as a deck from now on.

A modern deck doesn't need to be as complicated as you think, as early-stage plans are clearly simpler (versus later-stage ones, where the company has scaled operations and profits). The purpose of a plan or deck is to help you craft how you communicate your business and to provide interested investors with the extra information they need to evaluate your company after meeting you. No one has the time to read overly long or complicated decks, and for those investors who demand more data... well, perhaps ask them which areas they'd like more information on and you can deal with them on a case-by-case basis or send them a follow-up.

If you need inspiration, there are plenty of examples out there, from Guy Kawasaki's[4] *Art of the Start*[5] to ample examples of how other startups have crafted their decks (including

---

[4] http://www.guykawasaki.com/

[5] https://guykawasaki.com/books/the-art-of-the-start/

RewindAI, Brex, and LinkedIn). Additionally, TechCrunch published an article[6] that captures amazing stats about what works and what doesn't in terms of decks (the article is from 2015, but makes the point!).

Any plan/deck should, at the bare minimum, include:

1. **A clear representation of the problem you are solving and for whom.** Knowing your customer, why they need what you offer, and why you will rise to the top of their mind is critical to convey quickly.
2. **An overview of who you are** and what you've done (basically, why you and your team can make this happen).
3. **A succinct explanation of what your product/service does.** Use screenshots if possible; run it past a non-techie friend and see if they can explain it back to you.
4. **A market overview section**. The market size of your opportunity (what you can capture from incumbents in particular, if relevant), key players, competitors, partnerships, target market[7], and so on.
5. **Your financials and commercial traction to date**. Armed with your milestones from the earlier section, this will effectively showcase how you will use your cash. This section will require you to highlight how you think you will make and use money raised. If your business is about growth first, clearly show your potential investors how much money you will need to grow the company to where it hits the tipping point. It goes without saying that if you have traction, show it, but make sure you also have

---

[6] http://tcrn.ch/1BaFZfl

[7] http://en.wikipedia.org/wiki/Target_market

a good walk-through on how you acquired it, as costs of acquisition are as important as any top-line revenue those customers might generate!
6. **Competitive differentiation.** How you bring value to your customers (the pain points) as well as how you differentiate from competitors in your market.

All decks typically cover baseline information, such as identifying your market and competitors. Naturally, depending on the type of company you are, you will prioritize different parts of the story over others. If you have a wide technical moat and an excellent team, you'll talk about this more than commercial elements you may not have. Regardless, no matter how short a deck is, it is useful for investors evaluating an opportunity. It also offers value to founders in preparing it because it helps them articulate the core concepts of product, market, opportunity, the team, and the investment proposal.

Remember, a deck/plan is about organizing your thoughts and conveying them clearly to someone else, not about meeting some magical quota of pages with graphs and charts.Although, depending on the complexity of your proposition, this may be necessary.

Generally speaking, I have found a company's deck/plan has allowed me to determine:

1. The company's **communication style** and ability to articulate what they (their product or service) do, clearly and succinctly. Does the company rely too much on buzzwords and/or comparisons to get the point across, or are objectives and vision clearly discernible? Is it well written and free of grammatical errors? When I walk away

from reading it, can I describe the opportunity in simple terms to others? How do they use visuals? What kind of style does the company have? Terrible decks can still convert, but do you really want to take that chance?

2. The founder and their team's **ability to research** their **market size, competitors, key industry players, distribution channels, etc**. If a company has not adequately researched the size of their market, this can be a real deal-killer. I remember once meeting founders of a new company, and while I was originally really excited about the potential for their product, pointed questions during our meeting revealed that the market size was only a few million dollars worldwide. As you can imagine, deducing the size of your market during an investor meeting is probably not the best way to make an impression. Make sure you truly understand your target market, and the key players within it.

3. The **identification and articulation of differentiation from key competitors** is an important detail to include and can actually play in your favor if you can clearly articulate how you differentiate yourself. In the case of some companies, where distribution channels and key partnerships are important, identifying these and discussing them is important to provide potential investors with confidence that your team understands the challenges inherent to its industry.

4. The company's ability to **analyze its cash needs and expectations for growth**. Nothing is scarier than a company whose ambitions are huge, but whose idea of cash management is not in line. As we covered during the milestones section, you don't need a CFO, but you do need

to have thought out what key costs will grow with your ambitious growth and when the crucial cash-points are for your company. Generally speaking, investors don't have financial discussions at the very first meeting, but thoroughly understanding your cash uses will make you seem far more competent.

5. The completeness and **experience of the company's team**. Suffice it to say, if you have a great team, highlight their accomplishments. If you know you need to hire someone to round out your team, it's okay to put that down as a future hire—at least the investor will know that you know there is a weak point in the team, and that you plan on solving it as soon as the investment comes in.

On the subject of your team, don't underestimate the importance of your team's slide. When an investor considers your company at its earliest stages, **who you are (effectively your team) is just as important as your idea, if not more so**. Your team is a crucial part of your company's success. Yet, many founders make two critical errors: they either omit their team slide — failing to present them — to focus on the product or, bludgeon it because they don't feel they have anything interesting to add other than team photos and job descriptions.

What's worse is when founders just point to the team slide during a pitch, and say something like "Here is our team, we have lots of rockstars"—or something generic like that.

Let's look at what the major selling points of a team slide should be:

1. **A team's depth of experience**. Basically, does your team know anything about what you are doing? If you are

a healthcare company, do you have a healthcare background? If you are making something for the financial industry, have any of your team members worked in it? Does the team have the right connections across the value chain you operate in to deliver what you say you will deliver? What companies have your team members worked for that can validate you? If you've worked at Google, for example, it would be worthwhile to put that company logo up on your team slide because the image of the brand would speak faster to your audience than any number of words you could say in the same time frame.
2. **A team's capacity to deliver.** Are you effectively complete or incomplete as a team? Is your team mostly business people but lacking the technical capabilities to deliver, or is your team well rounded and able to execute? If your company industry requires an amazing specialist, do you have that specialist? By the way, do not assume its a bad thing to admit, if asked, that you are looking to hire for specific functions you don't currently have internally; doing so shows maturity and self-awareness —although you don't have to state it as part of your pitch.
3. **A team's culture and communication style**. What is your company like? Is it a fun place to work or is the tone more serious? What "titles" do people have? How many of your team are outward-facing and how many inward-facing?

As for where your team slide should sit within the deck, there is no hard-and-fast rule. I've found that if you are building something born out of a personal experience at your prior job, it makes for a decent early slide to explain the backstory to your pitch. If you are building something unrelated to your

- **Fully diluted amounts.** Whenever an investor says they want 5 percent of your company on a "fully diluted basis", it means that all promised equity (employee options included) are taken into account in the calculations so that they're effectively getting 5 percent at the end of the day.
- **Pre-money valuation.** When people generally talk about the valuation of a company, they're usually talking about the pre-money valuation—effectively, the company's worth prior to the new investment coming in. In a later chapter, we will discuss how companies can be valued in greater detail.
- **Round size.** The amount of money being raised representing your projected cash needs to achieve your stated milestones.
- **Post-money valuation.** The sum of the pre-money plus the round size. If the pre-money valuation of a company is $20 million and the founders raise $5 million from investors, their post-money valuation would be $25 million. Investors would therefore own 20 percent ($5 million / $25 million) on a fully-diluted basis. Your post-money valuation "sets the bar" for your future activities. If your post-money after your first round of financing is $4 million, you know that to achieve success in the eyes of your investors, any future valuations will have to be in excess of that amount. If subsequent rounds are valued at exactly $4 million, that's called a "flat round." Valuations below the post-money of the last round are called a "down-round". No one likes a down-round.

In case you are wondering, further on in this book, ASAs, SAFEs and convertible notes are covered!

The Fundraising Equation

If you take the values from the above calculations, you get a functional equation to determine what percentage of your company an investor will own post-investment (assuming they are the only investor in the round). The equation is quite simple, and you'll recognize it as I've mentioned it before:

round size/post-money valuation = the investor(s) ownership percentage

If you really want to geek out on valuations, A16Z has some great resources here: https://a16z.com/tag/valuation-and-valuations/

The Option Pool

Creating a cap table will likely entail an employee option pool (I'm avoiding the technicalities between the different variants of these, such as Restricted Stock Units, for simplicity's sake). **Unfortunately, the option pool is one of the most complicated parts of your company's cap table and, from the founder's point of view, can be very confusing because of how investors expect it to be treated.**

In simple terms, an option pool is merely a carve out from your existing shareholder's shares to accommodate new and future employees, directors, and advisors. As a general rule, employees in the same role who joined your startup earlier will receive a larger percentage of the option pool than employees who join later.

Where it gets confusing is in how you calculate the pool and the size it should be. In terms of how large the typical option pool is, well, it varies. I've seen it range from as low as 5 percent to as high as 20 percent depending on the company's stage and upcoming hiring needs as well as if they're based in the US vs. the EU. Typically, however, no matter how large the option pool is, it is generally spoken of and calculated on a "fully diluted basis". This means that investors are expecting a 10 percent option pool after their money has come in and all shares are accounted for. In order to achieve this outcome, the option pool needs to be calculated before their money hits the ledger, so to speak—effectively on a pre-money basis. If you want to go deeper into how this is calculated and why, search for the "Option Pool Shuffle". In summary, the important point is that the norm is for investors to expect your option pool to come out of the pre-money valuation of your company.

Index Ventures has created a very helpful tool to guide you through thinking about option issuance and size, which can be found here: Index Ventures Option Plan.

There are many great online tools to help you build your cap table. As useful as these can be to get started, nothing compares to you building your own cap table to get a feel for how future rounds, including those with convertibles, warrants, options for future employees, etc. can affect your and your investors' economics. By doing cap tables manually, much like driving a stick shift, you get a better feel for the impact different deals will have on your company. Once you are able to internalize this, you'll be far quicker and more effective when negotiating with potential investors, as you will be able to visualize the impact of their suggestions on your economics. If you want to see what a cap table looks like and use one as a starting point, my colleague Felix I created a set of videos that walks you through one, the links are available in the additional resources section of this book.

One final note on cap tables: cap tables can become toxic over time. What this means is that your cap table has become weighed down by external capital to a point where you and your team have become too diluted for what is considered "market" and thus, it will become difficult for you to raise additional funds without reconfiguring your cap table somehow.

The problem with toxic cap tables is that, except for obvious cases, they are largely a subjective measure determined by new investors. For example, raising money at the seed stage when you personally own 20 percent of the company is clearly toxic, but at what point does it become OK exactly? Toxic Rounds are covered in more detail in chapter 12 but, to provide you with some clarity, suppose you're not even at the Series A raise and you can see that you're headed to a situation where investors will own more than 40 percent of your company. I you're not already in a toxic situation, you will be quite soon.

6

The Power of Storytelling

Now that you are armed with the right mindset, knowing how much you want to raise and what your deck should look like, the final point is how to weave them together into one compelling narrative that captures the "why" and "how" of what you are building.

A founder's ability to communicate their vision and mission effectively is critical to their success. While a solid business plan and innovative ideas certainly play crucial roles, it is the art of storytelling that can truly captivate external parties and inspire them to join the journey. By harnessing the power of storytelling, founders can paint a vivid picture of their vision, allowing potential colleagues and investors to emotionally connect with their purpose. Failure to recognize and invest time in understanding this power can lead to frustration, as founders may find themselves wondering why others succeed while they struggle. Thus, for aspiring founders, mastering the skill of storytelling becomes an essential tool in their arsenal, enabling them to convey their dreams with clarity, passion, and a magnetic allure.

This section focuses on two aspects of fundraising storytelling: defining your vision and mission, and "how to tell it". Let's focus first on vision and mission and then discuss storytelling.

I was chatting with a friend recently about what makes some companies truly great while others are commercially successful but don't define a category. It's a tough question to answer and unpack with a single root cause, but in an effort to identify one, and as a thought exercise, I think it starts with the basics of why a company exists. It's vision.

Before getting into it, though, I want to say I cringe a little when I hear the terms "vision statement" and "mission statement" because we have all read many bland, unrepresentative, and over-hyped versions of each. They are usually on some plaque or in an "About Us" section of a website and even employees cringe a little when they read them because of how disconnected they can seem from reality. That said, this doesn't diminish their value if implemented correctly, or at least the thought exercise behind each. It just showcases how damn hard it is to get it right and truly mean it. One mission statement stands out for nailing it, for example, is Stripe's: "To increase the GDP of the internet".

So, in an effort to unpack the distinction between the two and show what well-implemented mission and vision statements can look like, I recall how inspired I was by what Nims Purja achieved with his Project Possible (now a feature film available on your favorite streaming platform).

In the mountaineering world, Nims Purja is a name that evokes admiration. The former Gurkha soldier is the holder of several mountaineering records, including the feat of summiting all 14 of the world's 8,000-meter peaks in just over six months, which he called project Possible. This record-breaking achievement was documented in the movie *14 Peaks*.

While Nims' mission as a mountaineer could have been simply to climb mountains to the best of his ability, what made him stand out was his vision of how to use those skills. It was not just to climb the mountains, but to do it in a way that had never been done before, to break the record of the fastest time to climb all 14 of the world's 8,000-meter peaks. This vision required him to think beyond the mundane and push the limits of what was considered humanly possible (the last person that did it took 8 years!).

So what's the difference between having a vision and a mission? Simply put, a mission is what you do and how you do it, and a vision is why you do it and what this means for your future. A mission statement is a short, concise statement that describes what an organization does, while a vision statement outlines its aspirations and goals.

It could be argued, in Nims' case, that his mission was to be the world's best mountaineer in the world. However, that might be defined as an aggregate of actions. For example, it could include achievements like the highest number of successful climbs, the most mountains climbed, or the single most technically complicated climb. These would have all been extensions of his mission, arguably "mini missions" in their own right.

However, the aggregation and culmination of all these 'missions' into the grander vision that became defined as *Project Possible* was his real vision. In effect, his vision was to do it (mountaineering) in a way that had never been done before, to set a new record of under seven months. Even the name of the vision —Project Possible — made a statement about how inconceivable the vision even seemed and yet how convinced he was in his ability to achieve it. Having a vision allowed him to expand his mission beyond the mundane and push himself and his team, to achieve something extraordinary and to prove to others that it could be done.

Nims Purja's story is an inspiring example of the power of having a vision. While his mission as a mountaineer could have been a simpler but still meaningful one (e.g., to climb mountains, assist others, write a memoir, etc.), his vision was to do it in a way that had never been done before and set a new record — it is a vision that ultimately is inspiring for us all. Having a vision allowed him to transcend his mission(s) and achieve something truly extraordinary. On a more 'tech' note, take Carl Pei, founder of Nothing and One Plus in crafting a powerful vision for what hardware can become beyond the incumbent narratives.

As you pursue your own goals and dreams for your companies, it's important to remember the importance of having a vision — to think beyond the mundane and push your teams to achieve something truly great.

Having a vision is crucial because it provides a sense of purpose and direction. It allows you to see the bigger picture, think beyond the day-to-day tasks and focus on what truly matters. When you have a vision, you are more likely to take risks and pursue your goals with passion and determination.

Now let's see how the storytelling element gets woven into the equation for fundraising. The art of storytelling involves the delivery of narratives and anecdotes to engage and connect with your audience, if you manage to entertain them along the way, that's even better. It includes the ability to captivate listeners or readers through your story's characters, descriptions, emotional arcs, and thought-provoking ideas and themes. Storytelling goes beyond simple information sharing; it engages the listener to feel, imagine, and create alongside you the storyteller. It taps into the universal human desire for meaning, connection, and understanding. This allows for ideas, values, and messages to be conveyed compellingly and memorably; which is why effective storytelling has the power to educate, motivate, and persuade particularly in the art of fundraising.

Continuing with the Project Possible analogy, Nims Purja had to fundraise for the expedition. If you've seen the movie or read the book, you will know that it was not easy. It never is, but he did it and what made it possible was his ability to explain the why behind his vision. In his words:

"I was told that my plan was impossible. So I decided to name it Project Possible...This is about inspiring the human race." He literally creates an emotional response of wanting the underdog to win and makes you want to root for their success.

In another interview in *Climbing* magazine, Nims says: "I've always known what I want to do [next] with my life. As a kid, I wanted to join Gurkhas. That was my only dream. When I joined the Gurkhas, I found out about the Special Boat Service, and that was my only dream. And after that, I just wanted to completely change the dynamic on 8,000-meter peaks — and that became my dream. So yeah, it's always specific. But one thing that all these dreams have in common is that I follow them."

Take note of his storytelling. Through what he says when talking about his achievement, we can guess that, in his fundraising pitch, he wove in the following facts

1 - He's doing this for a cause bigger than himself: to inspire the human race, to show what's possible, and to highlight the success of Sherpas in this sport.

2 - He's always been someone that takes on a challenge (i.e. Ghurkas, Special Boat Service, Mountaineering) and has come out the other end successfully.

3 - He's built the best team of experienced people to help him with his expedition.

4 - He's set a goal so ambitious that everyone will want to see him win as soon as they see that he's part of the way there, as everyone loves to root for an underdog overcoming insurmountable odds.

Those are all powerful storytelling tools which Nims no doubt used masterfully to recruit key team members, get support from family and friends, raise funds, get sponsors, and finally, even get a movie to tell the story. If that's not masterful storytelling, I don't know what is.

One final point on storytelling: English (or whatever language you're pitching in) doesn't need to be your first language.

As António R. Damásio famously said — *"We are not thinking machines that feel, we are feeling machines that think"*. Tap into that. Craft your vision, define your mission, and get incredibly good at telling their story!

7

The Human Element

The Best Way to Reach Investors

Getting in touch with an investor in a way that increases the likelihood that they'll reply is one of the most challenging things you'll have to learn quickly. That said, those interactions can also be some of the most rewarding parts of the fundraising process.

You'll develop fairly deep relationships with investors who become shareholders in your company. Trust me, the worst thing you can do is depersonalize your introduction by sending a vague, nondescript template email to ***info@investordomain*** that goes to no one. Remember our dating analogy? Well, sending an email like that is the equivalent of walking into a singles bar and announcing loudly, "HI, SINGLE PEOPLE. HERE AND READY TO MINGLE. I'LL BE AT THE BAR." Not a great way to promote the kind of intimacy you're looking for in either scenario. Instead:

1. **Research the investor and their firm.** It's a huge waste of time for you (and them) to reach out to someone who invests in the wrong sector, geography, or stage of your business. Review their website. Read about what they are interested in, professionally and personally. This will make your interaction with the investor far more relevant.
2. **Rely on a third party for an introduction**. If you can find someone who knows the person you're trying to reach, a personal introduction will serve you far better than trying to reach the investor in question directly. LinkedIn is a useful tool to find out who within your network knows the person you'd like to get in touch with. This makes the introduction process far more relevant.
3. **Keep your initial email short and to the point**. Don't overdo it content-wise and length-wise. You don't want the investor to glance at the sheer mass of your email and relegate it to the "to read" bucket. I've seen some

well-intended emails that were so tediously long that they were more off-putting than anything. This only creates a massive cognitive wall to overcome before an investor is even sure they are interested in pursuing further.

As a start, keep it to no more than three paragraphs. If you can't reach out to someone and explain in three paragraphs what you do and why it matters, there are bigger issues you may have in how you tell what you do. Secondly, avoid playing games with information you share, just be up front, what you are working on, who you are, what your connection is to the investor (if there is one), and how much you are raising.

If you want to add more, add it as an attachment so that once someone gets what you are doing from the main body of your email, they can read more.

4. **Think of your initial email as merely a preview or elevator pitch** with a call to action, such as asking them to reply or call if they are interested in the idea and want more information.
5. **Don't forget to thank the person who introduced you** and feel free to keep them updated on the conversation, but remove them from the cc of the initial intro email (move them to bcc). You don't want to overburden their inbox either!
6. **Twitter (X), LinkedIn, Reddit, Threads, Insta, and other social media.** are increasingly becoming efficient tools for contacting people for quick things, if used sparingly and in a very specific, non-generic way. You can @reply someone you are interested in to engage in a conversation or comment on what they said as a starter. Avoid sweet-talking though.

7. **Get out of the office.** Go to events (online or in-person) and make new friends! At the start, a lot of it will be hit-and-miss and feel like a waste of time, but you will start calibrating good events and people from those that are less in line with what you need. Don't hesitate to start being more selective once you've referenced events and people better. When attending, find people to introduce you to others to avoid interrupting ongoing conversations. Don't be afraid to work your way into the conversation if they are open to it and you feel that you can make a valuable contribution. If the person you want to meet seems engaged, back away and come back later. Remember, you might be a relief to the conversation they are having, but you don't want to be the distraction either. Feel it out, but don't be afraid to take the risk of speaking up—and when you do, get to the point quickly. You have about 30 seconds to make your conversation with someone—anyone—relevant to them. If an investor gives you feedback during this conversation, the worst thing you can do is come across as defensive. That will make you stand out for all the wrong reasons.

Remember, it's the job of investors to find amazing companies. If you're amazing, they're likely to be just as eager to meet you as you are to meet them. However, they are also very time-starved and don't want to waste time on opportunities that don't pique their interests. For further reading on how to get a meeting with investors, read Robin Klein's Medium post on the matter, "Getting your foot in a VCs door" (check the additional resources section for full-length links).

Invest in Yourself

Because building relationships is so crucial to the fundraising process, I have consistently seen good relational skills make a big difference for founders. This is not only the case when fundraising; it is also relevant when finding employees, clients, and partners for their company. The old adage, "It's not what you know, but who you know", is very much consistent with what I've observed over the years. Considering that you are the biggest factor in your ability to build relationships, a substantial investment in yourself is needed to fine-tune this essential aspect of fundraising.

If you are the kind of person who panics at the idea of meeting and speaking with lots of new people at startup events, there are many ways to practice that can hopefully ease your pain. Let's take a look at a few:

1. The easiest place to start is the **self-learning route**, with two books I rank very highly: *Never Eat Alone* by Keith Ferrazzi and *The Charisma Myth* by Olivia Fox Cabane. These books will help you understand many of the social cues necessary for you to effectively network. They also do a good job explaining the "why" of all things social, which is necessary for you to understand and internalize before going out and practicing your skills. These are must-reads. "Charisma on Command" by Charlie Houpert on YouTube is also a good resource to see it 'live'.
2. Next, if you want to step it up a bit, **engaging with a professional coach** can help you understand how to overcome some of the challenges that prevent you from networking effectively. These days, having a coach shows

strength in that you're actively investing in developing yourself. A coach doesn't necessarily set goals for you, but helps you understand what steps to take to achieve what you set out to achieve, considering all the variables you may have in play. Coaching works, but make sure you understand what kind of coach you are looking for, as coaching as a practice, is not homogeneous.

3. Try programs like Toastmasters which can help with public speaking skills.
4. Lastly, the most extreme step is to push the boundaries of your personality with something that takes you out of your comfort zone so that you can learn how others see you. One example is to enroll in **an improvisational comedy course**. I did it and tried out imprology.com here in London. Boy, was I in for a surprise. It was as close to shock therapy as I'll probably ever come. But it gave me a crash course in some of the social dynamics that connect us to others that we frequently forget about or ignore when out socializing. Oh, and if you think improvisational comedy is all about telling jokes, you couldn't be further from the truth— I don't think we told a single joke during the entire program. It was more about learning to read others and reacting to their social signals with intention (vs. unintentionally, which can happen quite easily if you are unaware of social queues). An example of a social queue is when someone clearly appreciates being 'right'.. so how do you acknowledge which parts of what they said 'might be right' before your establish your view? This intentional approach prevents people from closing up prematurely to what you might say.

Thus, following from the above, a key concept that arose during the improvisation course was how to **amplify other people's emotional offers and not reject them at the start.** Many times we are too closed in the way we converse. We don't pay attention to how others are reacting or what they might be suggesting, perhaps because we are too busy thinking about what to say next! Improvisation teaches us how to interpret people's emotions first, follow through with them, and explore what they may lead to before injecting our own ideas into an interaction.

Another key concept in improvisation is **understanding the inherent social status** we all have relative to each other and how they can change in different circumstances. Violating status hierarchies can drastically affect how others perceive you, in an extreme example, imagine not addressing a royal individual by their title? You'd come across as rude! Whilst taking an improv course to learn these ideas might be a bit radical, it can help tie various social concepts together, for those with very tight time commitments, however, the accompanying book to the course I took, *Impro* by Keith Johnstone, is also an amazing read that walks through all the key concepts; you just miss out on practicing them in person!

In the end, all of this takes practice, time, and patience. Practicing these concepts and dealing with the anxiety you will naturally feel as you experiment, will help you **identify social offers** that others give you to engage with them. There are no shortcuts. You'll spend a lot of time trying to cultivate relationships, and you won't always achieve the outcomes you anticipated. If you are going to work on these skills and they don't come naturally to you, it will take perseverance and patience with yourself to overcome the natural anxieties you feel. One thing that was constantly said during improvisation class was "Don't beat yourself up". We are all our own worst critics.

8

The Search for an Investor

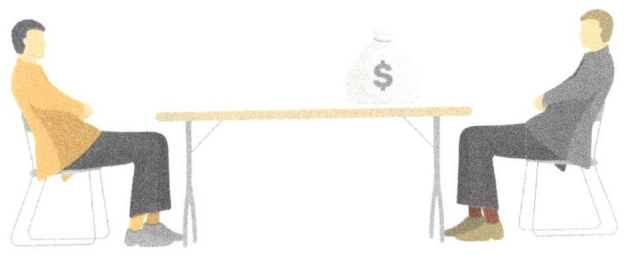

Investor Rankings vs. Reality

I am often asked by founders to help identify the ranking or 'tier' (i.e., tier 1, 2, etc.) of a prospective investor, with the founders assuming that the higher the 'tier' of an investor, the more it will drive the likely success of a company. However, I don't think this is the best way to approach an investor search. While this assumption holds true to some extent, it is more of a correlation than causality.

In other words, **the success or failure of your company depends mostly on you, not on your investor's brand**. What great investors do is identify great founders and support them on their journey. Hence, a correlation exists over time. Sadly, this correlation, and the many publications that show these correlations through rankings of investors, exclude many new/emerging funds and funds that don't share public information about their companies. These rankings also obscure the reality of how nuanced a founder's experience can be within the same fund versus another founder's experience. So, while these lists, rankings, and tiers can be great starting points for your search, they are flawed as they exclude many investors who have specialty knowledge or experience that could be invaluable for you and your team. The very best way to approach a search is by finding the right investors with attributes that suit you.

Investor Attributes

Below are the seven attributes that I believe differentiate the best from the rest. As you seek out potential investors, keep an eye out for these characteristics— the more of these your prospective investor has, the better off you will likely be as a founder.

1. **Can "flex" a great network**. The biggest value-add that an investor can bring to the table is their network. The larger their network, the more doors they can open for you. Nothing beats a direct intro to someone you need to meet, whether it be for hiring purposes, potential customers, or

for follow-on capital.
2. **Has a great brand name.** This helps with introductions, but having an investor with a great brand name, either as an individual (usually the case for new funds but also older funds) or fund (usually the case for more established funds), can help open doors. Whether indirectly (as in, not requiring an introduction) or directly, reputable funds provide your startup with instant validation to potential customers, partners, and new investors.
3. **Has sufficient levels of capital to support you**. Although different investors have different strategies around this (i.e. an angel can rarely follow on as much as an institutional fund), it is generally a good thing to have an investor who can invest in your company throughout its life cycle. The age of the fund has a large part to play in this. The older the fund, the less likely it is to have as much capital available.
4. **Has sector expertise**. One way that investors can differentiate themselves as a top-tier investor from the usual suspects is by having focused experience in your sector. For example, an investor could be a generalist Tier 2 fund (remember that this is subjective), but as an e-commerce investor they may be Tier 1—great if you are an e-commerce company, but just okay if you're a fintech company. This is because they will likely have a large network in their sector of expertise.
5. **Has deal experience**. You will go through a lot of unique and stressful situations during a fundraise. It helps to have someone who has gone through the process before and can help smooth things out between all parties involved, if needed.

6. **Isn't burdensome.** Sometimes the best action an investor can take is simply get out of the way. An excellent investor does not burden the founder during the investment process with unnecessary or unusual diligence requirements for the stage the company is at. For example, a company that is very early-stage will likely not have much to be "diligenced." If an investor requires you to have an accurate vision of what will happen in your company five years from now and you started your company three months ago, question whether they truly think the information you will give them has any likelihood of being true (and whether you think they'd make a good investor for you).
7. **Is a visionary.** Good investors on your board will advise you on best practices for company building. Great investors will help you set the right vision for your company. Better investors help you think big because they think big themselves. They have a=can-do (vs. can-not) attitude and the experience to coach you through this type of thinking.
8. **Lastly, and most importantly, you get along.** To clarify, your goal should not be to find a new best friend, but rather someone you don't hate talking to, fear, or respect simply because of the brand name they represent. Having an investor you feel comfortable talking to can be a huge asset when dealing with the highs and lows of early startup life. If it is a healthy relationship, they can also serve for emotional support in tough times and a Socratic and understanding sounding board in general.

With this list of key investor qualities in mind, consider:

- There are many new investment funds and/or individual angels that enter the ecosystem and may not have established brand names, but have great networks and experience. Don't dismiss them prematurely; however, do ask others they've worked with what it's like to work with them.
- Although founders who have done well and gone on to join a fund can be awesome people to have on your board, investors don't have to have been founders themselves to be great investors (e.g. Fred Wilson of Union Square Ventures). Experience as an investor—someone who has done many deals and knows how the best companies operate—can count for a lot. So, look for a blend of all attributes in your investor and not just a founder-turned-investor that can empathetically relate to what you're going through.
- If you're ever stuck between two potential investors, consider that the person who will be working with you on the board will help you define many things about your company over the coming years. Choose wisely and ask yourself who you would rather work with long-term. You wouldn't want to choose someone solely for a good brand if they cause you hair loss, heartburn, and emotional stress on a regular basis.

As always, do your due diligence on your investor. If possible, and the opportunity presents itself to request it, ask to speak to their portfolio company CEOs to see what value the investor brought to the table for them.

The Typical Institutional VC Investment Process

VC firms' investment processes vary too much to think of them as standardized. There are corporate funds, funds backed by professional investors called "limited partners", evergreen funds (that typically invest from their balance sheet), angel syndicates, and family funds—just to name a few. These funds may operate under deal-champion partnerships, unanimous decision partnerships, and investment committee-heavy partnerships, and naturally all sorts of variants in between. The details of these are not relevant for this book, but with so much variance among investors and their processes, what is the best way to know where you stand in a VC's process?

First and foremost, do your research. You can do a lot of it online and/or via connections. Here is a list of questions/factors to look for:

- **Historical Research**—Search on Crunchbase, AngelList, etc. Find out what they've done, who they've done it with, and how they've done it. This might also highlight biases they have towards sectors.
- **Portfolio.** Research their portfolio of companies and see if you know any of the CEOs. If you do, or know someone who does, have a chat with them to understand how the fund works and how their investment decision process works.
- **People.** Research the partner and associate you will be talking to. The more you know about them, the better you can tailor your message to their area of investment interest. You also want to get a feel for whether you want to work with them in the first place!
- **Competitors.** Find out if they have invested in your com-

petitors, which is always difficult to do, but usually more obvious with later-stage funds or multi-stage funds that will have made a bet on a sector already. Typically earlier-stage funds know that companies change and evolve, so they will likely be open to reviewing your company even if there is some minor overlap.
- **Fund Age:** Find out how old their fund is, as older funds will likely be less willing to take very high-risk investments or might be out of cash entirely.
- **Speed:** How fast do they do deals, will they need to take weeks because they need to get multiple layers of approvals or can they turn things around in days because they have a much lighter internal process? For example, some funds might have a two week partner-centric cerebral discussion vs. an insight-driven associate-led VC firm might want very swift DD on a Saturday evening.

Once you know who you're dealing with and have secured a first meeting, don't be afraid ask further questions to clarify this particular firm's process: "What's your firm's investment process?" "How do you usually work with companies?" "What's our next step? How should I follow up?"

Let's imagine a typical venture capital fund might have various steps prior to an investment decision (assume the example below begins with an associate rather than a partner. If meeting with a partner, the process might be faster, but don't dismiss associates):

- **First Meeting**. Mostly kicking the tires and trying to get a feel for the founders, but also the size of the opportunity.
- **Second Meeting**. A follow-up on information requested

from the first meeting. These days this might be skipped earlier in your journey as rounds are moving faster and faster.
- **Meeting with a Partner.** In cases where the above two meetings were with an associate or analyst but only partners can close deals (not always the case), this might be when the associate feels confident enough about the opportunity to present it to the partner they believe will champion the deal internally.
- **Meeting with all the Partners.** If a partner has been involved from the beginning, you might cut straight to this phase if all is going well, but either way, meeting with everyone at the same time signals a key moment for the partnership to make a decision about the investment.
- **Investment Committee.** Some funds need investment committee (the supervisors of the partnership, if you will) approval on deals as a second layer. This might be a very light or heavy process and may potentially block a deal that a partnership wants to do.

In the end, the best thing to do is to inform yourself about the process as much as you can before and during your first meeting so that you have more certainty about how to navigate the rest of the process going forward.

Meeting with Non-Partners in a Fund

This is one area that I want to double-down on because there are a lot of opinions on this matter and many of them in my view are unnecessarily polarizing and downright insulting at times.

There is this perception in our ecosystem that only meetings with partners in a fund matter. Perhaps it is because partners are usually the ones on a fund's investment committee and thus are usually the ones making the decisions. While true, partners are also likely to be quite busy with other things on a day-to-day, such as fund administration and people management and so, they rely on and TRUST their more junior team members.

Analysts, associates, and principals are sometimes dismissed by founders as not worth talking to because someone on the internet said they aren't ultimately the decision-makers, so why waste your time on them? Well, having been an analyst and associate myself earlier in my career, I can tell you a few things about how junior members of an investment team think:

1) If you hate a founder because of how they made you feel, you can easily prevent a company from making it into the investment review process of your fund.
2) If you love a founder because of how they made you feel, you can easily lobby for a company to be prioritized for the next review process. At Seedcamp, I can tell you we've made plenty of decisions based on the recommendations of our analysts and associates!

Yes, perhaps decision-making might not fall in their remit, but as discussed earlier in the book, this is a people business. I suggest you treat all interactions with team members of a fund as opportunities to build relationships within that fund. Don't be so desperate to optimize for a specific person within a fund so early on that you sideline the very person who is championing you in the first place.

How Does an Investor Review Your Team?

Earlier, we discussed the importance of your team to an investor. A startup's founding and management team is a company's lifeblood. No amount of awesome ideas will ever overcome a fundamentally flawed management team. In the early stages of any startup, success is all about the people.

But what makes up a good team? How do you know if you have a good team, if you are a good team member, and if an investor will perceive your team the way you perceive them?

A good team is comprised of people whose personality attributes include a combination of confidence, stubbornness, individuality, a sense of self without arrogance, curiosity, humility, energy, maturity, a record of solving tricky problems together and apart, and an overall eagerness to learn. I have also found that founders who possess many of these characteristics tend to fare better over the long term than those who don't.

But a good team is more than just a collection of star personalities. Investors will analyze your whole team to find:

1. **Technical or commercial competency.** This can mean the founder(s) have relevant experience from having done a startup before, have performed well in their previous role(s) or, they have developed the appropriate skills necessary to execute on the company's stated vision.
2. **Quick, constructive conflict resolution**. Roadblocks are inevitable along the startup journey, and knowing how to cope improves the forecast of your team's longevity. Knowing when to crack a joke, divide a problem into parts, or take a break can mean the difference between staying

together or falling apart. Although I have heard of some investors doing an artificial stress test during investment reviews, it isn't standard practice. A seasoned investor can usually tell just from spending time with a team whether internal personality conflicts are at play.

3. **Intuition about when to persevere or quit.** Some people quit too early; others keep going beyond the point at which a strategy stops working. Those that take too long to quit burn too much cash beyond a point of being able to pivot effectively or having the option of returning funds to investors. This quality is harder to evaluate than others, but if you can demonstrate awareness of this—perhaps by citing a time when your team pivoted from one strategy to another—you'll be able to show your potential investor that you'll use his time and money wisely.

4. **An understanding of the assumptions and metrics of the market** they wish to operate in, or at least an understanding of how to research this information. Every great team I've ever met has understood the dynamics of their market, known what information/data they needed to gather and how to analyze that data to determine if they were going down the right path.

5. **The team or founder can articulate their thoughts and plans.** Both internal and external communication is the most important thing to get right within an organization. You may have an awesome coder on your team, but if he doesn't understand what management is looking for, he can't produce something great. Externally, founders with an awesome product who can't communicate their vision to the outside world won't be able to interest others in joining their venture.

6. **A positive spirit of collaboration.** I believe that collaboration can be summarized as a combination of conflict resolution skills and communication skills. A team's ability to collaborate internally (with team members) and externally (with business partners, investors, and the media) greatly increases the chances that they will succeed.
7. **The geographical spread of a team.** Yes, Zoom, MSFT Teams, FaceTime and Google Meet have done marvels to revolutionize the way we communicate. But, for the necessary "collision of ideas" (borrowing from Steven Johnson's book on Where Good Ideas Come From[8]) to occur repeatedly, close physical proximity is an asset. That said, with the rise of remote work capabilities, if your team is spread out for a reason— as in you have hired the best from one geography— make sure you talk to investors about how you've thought through managing a remote work culture.
8. **The equity spread among founders.** Although generally speaking most founding teams have an equal equity spread (50/50, 33/33/33, etc.) and there is no 'right formula', an investor will take note if there is an equity imbalance that may potentially make a key hire or co-founder feel unmotivated.

When I meet a startup's management team, I look at the eight attributes listed above and ask myself three questions:

---

[8] http://www.ted.com/talks/steven_johnson_where_good_ideas_come_from

- Does this team have the necessary experience it takes to deliver what it has set out to do? (Teams with technical founders are of particular interest to me.)
- Does this team have the insight to identify its own weaknesses and hire good people to complement them?
- Can this team constructively deal with all the challenges that will occur during the company's life cycle?
- Can this team inspire investors to believe in them?

If you're considering creating a company or are already fundraising, think about what skills you and your team members have, and make sure you can articulate when and how you will hire for the deficiencies. Additionally, if you're a single founder, it helps to find a co-founder with complementary skills.

Ultimately, what makes a good team is subjective and, in my experience, the more subjective a question's answer is, the better off you are getting various opinions in order to triangulate the answer. To that end, I asked some industry colleagues what they look for in a team. Below, you can find some of their answers.

> *Luciana Lixandru, Sequoia Capital*
> *For us, the earlier we meet a founder the better, so it's often a state of mind or an attitude that makes a first impression. We like outliers—people who question the status quo and are convinced they can make it better. At Sequoia, we're looking for founders who want to build enduring companies and it's important they are thinking on a global scale from very early on.*

I also love to see depth of knowledge—founders who are so motivated to solve the problem, they come at it from every possible angle. The more you dig and ask questions, the clearer it becomes that they have unparalleled understanding of their customer, market and product. There is no one size fits all, but these things, coupled with a deep-rooted need to win, can be a very powerful combination.

Judith Dada, La Famiglia
I look for a team that is eager to grow in everything they do and through the people around them. Some of the best founders I have met somehow turn everyone they meet into an asset for them, but without people feeling used. They see the interactions with employees, partners, and experts as opportunities to grow—both themselves and the business. As an investor, they'll answer your questions confidently, providing insight generously and honestly, but then also pick your brain for the 1 percent new information that adds value to their own knowledge. They just have a natural knack for leveraging resources and multiplying them, with everyone growing in the process.

Robert Lacher, Visionaries Club
We are looking for founders with massive passion and contrarian ideas to reshape the industrialized world. Being a founder is not a job, it's a lifestyle, it defines you.
We thus love to back product driven founders who follow their deepest passion in what they are doing. Being truly

passionate about something is what gets the best out in you, it is what makes you hungry, fight and thrive every single day to make a dent building a category defining company, it is what gets you up in the morning – often through many ups and downs. Passion is typically the intersection of what you love doing and what you are good at. It is not always easy and often takes time to find out, for yourself and within a team. It requires to be brutally honest to yourself and not settle. We thus value teamwork over showmanship and strongly believe that taking ego out of the equation is the best basis to strive as a strong founding team. Eventhough a healthy dose of ego can be a strong driver for success :)

Carmen Rico, Cocoa

One characteristic common to all my investments is a very strong founder market fit: I look for founders that hold a secret on the market they are going after and that are fueled by relentless passion (almost an obsession) to solve the problem they are tackling. I have been a founder myself and looking back I think one of the reasons I failed was that I wasn't passionate enough about the problem I was trying to solve. So, now I look for true passion.

I also have a thing for data-driven founders—they grow much faster. Being data-driven allows you to know and control your business much better, i.e. it enables you to test and learn quicker and to identify and action your levers of growth earlier.

Leila Rastegar Zegna, Founding Partner, Kindred Capital

Our investment thesis is very much founder-led (vs. sector led). We always invest at the pre-seed and seed stage, and look for mission-driven founders who have an almost irrational hubris to them, and ambition levels that underpin their belief that they can genuinely change the way the world works with their technology, and want to build game-changing outcomes. Most of the founders we back have struggled (personally) with the problem that they're setting out to solve, and there is a very deep-rooted belief that their solution MUST exist in the world...and they'll never, never, never give up until they make it work. Missionary vs. mercenary. Often times headstrong and stubborn, but voracious for feedback and input, and hell bent on making a dent in the universe. In other words, we look for the very thin venn diagram overlap between seemingly contradictory traits: rational enough to execute, but irrational enough to build a category defining company... the ability to fly at 20,000 feet and 20 feet... giving all of the f*cks and none of the f*cks... highest of standards coupled with deepest devotion.... both killer, and kind.

Rytis Vitkauskas, Founding Partner, Dig Ventures

Starting a company is a 10+ year commitment. As a converted founder myself, understanding founders' genuine motivations and "why this, why now" is important. Aside from the rare combo of technical excellence and strong go-to-market DNA in a team, we tend to gravitate towards founders who are mature enough to be real in sharing what they know and don't know, capable of deep introspection, and are coachable. This doesn't mean the founder does what others say, but they have the capability and the need to listen and hear.

Unlike the more traditional Silicon Valley evaluation lens, at Dig Ventures we take limited signal from founders' formal employment or educational pedigree. We find that passion for the problem, unique insight and grit are better predictors of success.

Lastly, being a founder is the loneliest professional activity one could be doing. Too many co-founders in a company is not optimal, but 2 > 3 > 1 in this case and ideally founders know one another well + complement each others' skillsets.

Ivan Farneti, Five Seasons Ventures

Three ingredients seem to present in the teams we backed. It is not a precise recipe with exact weights and measure every time, but nevertheless three elements were always present: passion for the problem to solve, as measured by the depth of domain knowledge of the team; ambition to take on a large opportunity, even if complex, to build a big business; and a good mix of leadership/management skills, as teams need both to set the direction and execute it with precision and focus. When a startup possesses these three ingredients, raising capital shouldn't be too hard.

Carl Fritjofsson, Creandum

Building a world-class company takes time and requires an incredible range of skill. However, the one most important characteristic of a founder is a genuine and deep curiosity for what they're building. With curiosity comes the desire to constantly better understand your market, customers, and team. This is the extreme *level of details which drives founders to continuously challenge what they do and how they can better serve all stakeholders of their business. Curiosity creates the endless drive to iterate and improve, which is the fundamental DNA of long-term company creation.*

Sean Seton-Rogers, PROfounders Capital
Metrics are the most important for us: knowing your numbers cold, measuring everything. I'm all over that stuff. Seriously. You (and we) don't know what's going right or wrong if you're not measuring it. The remaining attributes we look for are really EQ based: "ability to sell a story" and "pitch a big vision", for example.

Jason Ball, Angel
I look for teams that innovate versus optimize. Innovation means a step change that can create an entire new category (and produce outsized returns for an investor). Optimization only improves an existing process or service through incremental gains (and subsequently produces mediocre investment returns). Most teams are only improving on what's already available, and calling it "innovation", when in reality it's only optimization...

Philipp Moehring and Andy Chung, Tiny.VC
People who work together on a startup should have some experience of spending time together before, ideally in a work setting where they were productive and successful together—at whichever level. Like in a sports team, they should play different positions and substitute deficiencies in each other to become a better whole.

Founding teams are the essence of a startup; they

create the culture, the product and the vision. As a founder and investor I look for a few things:

Passion for the problem—when things are tough, this is all you have left.

One tech co-founder—someone needs to be responsible for building the product.

History of creating value together—demonstrates compatibility and complementary skills.

Scott Sage, Crane Venture Partners
I look for founders who are deeply dissatisfied with the current solutions to a problem they are obsessed with solving. They know how to organize a story, attract the best and most diverse minds to join them, and constantly figure out how to add more value to their customers. On a personal level, I'm looking for people who are candid, open and looking forward to the daily challenge as a way to grow as a human being.

Alex Brunicki & Andre de Haes, Backed VC
We thought hard about this for years, but realize now there is no platonic ideal of a founder. Truly exceptional outcomes are engineered by those who are exceptions themselves. Nonetheless, three qualities will always stand out: industry fit (what is it about their personality, experience, skill-set that makes them uniquely well placed to win this market?), speed (how quickly do they make decisions under uncertainty?) and unbridled ambition.

Christoph Janz, Point Nine Capital
There are lots of "obvious" qualities a founder/manage-

ment team should have: they must know their market, they must be smart, they must be extremely dedicated, etc. This has been said a million times already of course, but that doesn't mean it's wrong.

To pick one quality which is particularly important from our point of view, the founders need to be able to build a kick-ass product that solves a real problem. As early-stage investors, we can and love to help in many areas, like sales, marketing, hiring, financing, etc., but the ability to create a great product with a clear product/market fit is something we believe needs to be in the founder team DNA.

Robin Klein, Localglobe
- Balance: product, technology, market/commercial.
- A leader in the team.
- Good mutual respect for one another.

Ophelia Brown, Founding Partner at Blossom Capital
I want to know why someone has chosen to dedicate every waking hour of the next 10 to 20 years to solve this one problem. Building a company is hard. There will be ups and downs. The highs make up for the lows, but the dark moments are real (I know this from building Blossom!), so I need to understand the passion, motivation and drive that will get them through these times. A founder living and breathing their company will be way smarter than me on the details of the problem—I want to learn from them and have them help inform my views. Finally, I also look for their leadership qualities—one person doesn't build a company, so I need to see that

they want and can attract top talent to the team.

Reshma Sohoni, my colleague at Seedcamp
We at Seedcamp really look for the "3 Ds" in terms of skill-set in a founding team—the Developer (the builder), the Designer (the product visionary) and the Distributor (the hustler)—whether that's all in one person or two, three, or four people doesn't matter. In terms of attitude it's all about that can-do hustle, the positive frame of mind, being helpful and giving to others, and showing confidence and gravitas.

Sitar Teli, Connect Ventures
I look at founding teams through two lenses: skill-set and founder/market fit. For skill-set, I look for a balance of skills amongst the founders in the following three areas: 1) design/UX, 2) marketing/distribution and 3) tech. They're all important, but relative importance depends on the industry the team is tackling. As for founder/market fit, I prefer founders who have a deep understanding or experience with the market they are building for.

Jeff Lynn, Founder - Co-Founder of Seedrs
When I look at teams that want to raise capital for their businesses through Seedrs, there are three key things I really focus on:

Product-Team Fit. We talk a lot in the startup world about product-market fit, but I think understanding the fit between the team and the type of company they're building is just as important. Are these the right people to build this particular type of company? Do they have the right experience and orientation for this particular field? Someone who could create an amazing SaaS enterprise play might not be the right person for a fashion-led e-commerce site, and vice-versa. I even use myself as an example: as a former lawyer and investor, there was a good fit for me to build Seedrs as a regulated financial services business; but had I set out to build a games business, when I haven't been a gamer since I was a teenager, the fit (and thus the likelihood of success) wouldn't have been there.

Hustle. I want to see teams who will get out there and do everything legal and ethical that it takes to be a success. Building a business is hard work, and while innate talent and intelligence are key, they'll get you nowhere unless you're willing to fight day-in and day-out to find customers, generate sales, form partnerships, ship product and, of course, raise funds. It's amazing how many smart people there are, even hard-working smart people, who expect success to come to them rather than realising that they need to push for every bit of it. This is especially important in the crowdfunding world—where the difference between a successful and an unsuccessful campaign is often about how well the team has activated their networks and created interest among their communities—but it applies to all aspects of building a successful business.

The Right Level of Insanity. The final thing I really care about is that the team be just insane enough to think they can take over the world without being so detached from reality that they won't do the hard work *to build their business. If the business is run by people who are completely focused on a narrow niche or a highly conservative growth strategy, it's unlikely to ever produce the kinds of returns that will be interesting to investors; meanwhile, if the team is such a group of dreamers that they're going to navel-gaze all day and can't focus on the nitty-gritty of gaining traction and raising funds, that's no good either. There is obviously a very fine line, and I've gotten it wrong on both sides in the past, but I think this "insanity test" a good way of thinking about the balance between ambition and practicality: the team should be one that really wants to shoot for the stars but knows that to get there you have to pass the moon first.*

How Does An Investor Review Your Financial Plan?

The financial plan, for most tech-focused, early-stage founders, is probably one of the most dreaded bits of the investment package to send your prospective early-stage investors.

As much as we'd like to think we can predict the future with all sorts of fancy extrapolations on growth rates like we did with milestones, the truth is we generally can't. Studies have shown[9] that people are just crap at predicting the future. They highlight success cases and bury failures, thus giving a skewed view of their ability to accurately predict outcomes. Considering that most people create financial projections based

---

[9] https://freakonomics.com/2011/06/30/the-folly-of-prediction-full-transcript/

on assumptions of what needs to happen for an upcoming month's worth of operating events and then project from there for x number of months or years, you effectively create a series of increasingly improbable chronological events with the last event (month) in the series being a function of the compounded set of decreasing probabilities, all of which are asymptotically approaching zero percent in their likelihood of happening "according to the plan".

What's my point? Well, that your financial plan isn't worth much from an accuracy perspective. So if that's true, you wonder, do I even bother?

In short, yes: **It's the detailed analysis of your thinking behind the model that gives an early-stage investor a feel for how you think and how you want to direct your company in the near future.** Second to that, how efficiently you use and plan to use cash to accomplish mutually agreed-upon goals will reveal much about you and your team.

I'm not going to discuss how you should format your financials, or explain basic accounting principles and how financial statements work. There are plenty of resources and tools online that can help you with that. Rather, I want to explore how an early-stage investor reviews the financial plan of an early-stage startup (vs. a later-stage startup, where there is a historical performance record with multiple years of budgets and actual figures). Effectively, I'm looking for the causes and effects of each number (ie, LTV, CAC, etc), and the key assumptions behind those figures. My discussion of financials with a founder or team will focus entirely on their assumptions and the reasoning behind them vs the expectations for them to be accurate in the future.

When an investor is discussing numbers with an entrepreneur, demonstrating a solid understanding of why the numbers are there, a clear view of the market dynamics in which their company operates, realistic customer acquisition assumptions and hiring plans, effective use of marketing budgets, and an understanding of the appropriate expenses for a growing company can have a HUGE impact on establishing the necessary credibility of competence an entrepreneur needs to inspire confidence. The opposite—seeing a financial plan with current month revenues and expenses projected five years into the future, assuming linear or exponential growth in all aspects of the organization and being presented it with a confident "this is what we realistically expect to happen"—can be demoralizing for an investor, if not outright humorous.

Let me share with you a little secret: with a few exceptions, you will always know your industry and its numbers better than any investor will. However, an experienced investor will ask you the right questions to ascertain whether or not you know your industry well enough to increase the probability of your own company's success. As such, **really do your homework**. And by that I mean, don't just go out and build a product and hope there will be customers. As soon as you have customer validation, make an effort to understand the market dynamics of that customer. How many of them are there? What is their concentration? How do you reach them? Are they locked in with a competitor with some sort of monthly or annual contract? Do they buy in a cyclical pattern? Do they prefer to buy online or only from salespeople? Do they need help setting up your product or can they use it as-is? What are they generally willing to pay for other similar services? How is the market growing? Mind you that in some circumstances, the ability to "charge" customers may not be deemed the real potential for revenues at first (think about Twitter when they were starting). But again, it's how you articulate the future value that matters.

If you take all those questions and research them, what you will find are key components of what will make up the assumptions on your future revenues (or value creation objective). Perhaps your customers are only willing to buy your product during the holiday season, so you will have a hard time during the off-season with less cash coming into your company. Financials that don't take that into consideration would look somewhat unrealistic to an investor, not in the numbers, but in the market dynamics of your product.

The more you can explain the reasons why a number in your financial model is based on a realistic set of assumptions, the better off you will be. But, look at it another way: by doing this exercise, you will realize whether your business is one that can actually make money (or some other method of value creation). For example, suppose you do the analysis and find that in the sector you are exploring, people aren't willing to pay and many competitors are giving the product away for free. You may have just saved yourself a serious amount of wasted energy!

Which brings us to the next part of the homework: **understanding your company's expenses.** If you have found a market where your product is actually capable of generating some sort of value, the next step is to figure out how to spend your money to match that customer growth. When do you hire new sales people and how many of them do you need? When do you bring new servers online, spend on marketing, spend on new offices, laptops, etc.?

Obviously the types and amounts of expenses vary from company to company, but what matters here is how they map to what you are trying to do and whether that mapping is realistic (what is your customer acquisition cost?). For example, if you have a marketing charge of $5000 one month for advertising, is it realistic to expect that next month your customer sign-ups will increase by 500 percent? Well, as I said before about the "dirty little secret"—an investor may have an idea, though perhaps not the exact details. But for sure they will expect you to explain how the $5000 will equal 500 percent growth.

The investor will evaluate your credibility based on the credibility of your answer. For example, if you answer, "I will buy $5000 worth of flyers and pass them out", you can rest assured that I will not believe your 500 percent growth figure. If however, your team's background has a track record of low-cost viral marketing campaigns, and your answer is basically a version of that... well, I might just find it plausible. I may be exaggerating the bit about an investor having "no flippin' idea", as most investors will have seen enough of what works and what doesn't to call you out on it. But again, if you can walk an investor credibly through your assumptions, it will do wonders for the confidence you create, particularly when your business may be trying to do things in a very different way than the investor may be used to.

Lastly and most importantly is the review of how the expenses map to the revenues as far as cash flow is concerned. Cash is a company's lifeline, and the biggest question for a founder is how much cash the company has before it either dies or needs to go fundraising again. As such, investors not only want to know how much a company needs in terms of cash to execute its vision, but also how that cash is being used. If there is a huge mismatch here, or there isn't enough time for you to reach your company's next milestone, this may be a point worth discussing.

THE SEARCH FOR AN INVESTOR

As you may have heard in the rumor mill, not all investors take projections seriously due to the inherently inaccurate nature of assumptions with little-to-no history behind them. One method investors sometimes use to figure out how much cash you need is to cut any revenue expectations you have anywhere from 50 to 100 percent to see how long your company can survive without any cash whatsoever. This is why it is so important for you to know what your monthly cash burn is and what your cash-out date is (when you run out). *A note to anyone who is leaving banking to start a company: your Jedi skills with a financial model might tempt you to go nuts with sensitivity tests and pivot tables and the like, but remember, less is more, particularly when dealing with unknown unknowns.*

With these shortcut numbers in mind, and a model built to allow an investor to test different scenarios (sensitivity analysis), you'll be further along in being able to come to an agreement as to how much cash your company may need to achieve your key milestones.

An additional resource relevant for this section is Founder Collective's article titled: "Why do VCs Really Want to See Your Financial Model? Hint: It's not about the numbers."

Further Questions You May Still Have On Your Search for New Investors

Can or should my existing investors help me navigate a future fundraise?

If you have existing investors, their shared connections can be a huge benefit in expanding the reach of your network. Tap into their networks and leverage their connections. Moreover, don't stop with just your investors; also prioritize connections from other founders and operators, as introductions from them can be just as powerful in opening doors, if not more, as they are not financially biased in the way your investors can be perceived to be.

Returning back to the question at hand: whilst intros from existing investors to future potential investors are generally positive, you should be mindful that, depending on the nature of your existing investor(s), it's not always obvious that an introduction is a good thing unless the existing investor is either 1) clearly not capable of leading your next round or 2) committing to participating in your next round. If they don't commit, then it can raise some flags for later stage investors.

To elaborate on the first point, let's focus on your angel investors or your pre-seed investors. For a new later-stage investor, it is clear that these earlier investors are likely not going to be able to write the check sizes that are required for them to lead a larger follow-on round (e.g., Series A), so their not participating won't necessarily generate a negative signal.

This is one of the benefits of taking investments from angels and stage-focused funds.

However, on the second point, assume a later-stage fund invested a small amount in your first round and they are known for seeking an approximate 15-20% ownership by (or before) the next round. Unless they lead the next round to 'make up' for them not owning their typical ownership stake, others could see this inaction as a clear negative signal. Alternatively, say this very same investor did commit in your seed round, but was able to get their ideal target ownership early— then a simple pro rata would be a good signal for any future lead investors.

In conclusion, don't hesitate to leverage the connections you have, investors or not. That said, do keep in mind that if you are using your investors' connections, who they are and what they plan on doing in your next round will affect the quality of those connections.

I'm increasingly getting approached by "scouts" from larger funds that want to invest in my round. Should I take their money?

Scout programs led by larger —and typically later stage— funds can be great. In theory, what they are doing is enabling experienced operators to write checks on their behalf. While this is a relatively new trend in Europe and limited to bigger funds, it is one I expect will continue to grow or evolve as an outreach model.

Scouts are typically experienced operators who help you, are aligned economically with your success and who give you access to downstream investors (and of course, primarily to the fund whose scout program they belong to). The only downside is, similar to relying on existing investors to make introductions for you, if the fund representing the scout doesn't 'lean in' at your next round, that could possibly be a negative signal. Naturally, if there is no track record of the fund leaning in in the past, this risk is diminished. Another 'con' of a scout associated with a larger fund is that they will of course, lobby on behalf of that fund if there is a discussion about how much pro rata to assign to their fund vs. other funds that might be of more use to you.

In summary, if properly vetted and considered, taking money from someone that participates in a scout program can be a good thing for you— just get clarity on the above points first.

If I had to choose between taking money from a Tier 1 fund (but a partner I didn't like as much) or a lower-tier fund (but a partner who I like more), which one should I prioritize?

First of all, if you're in this situation, congratulations— that's great! Secondly, if you are in a situation where you can build a syndicate with both parties involved (as in, one of them isn't pushing out the other), there might be a non-binary win:win outcome to this question.

However, what if it literally comes down to choosing between those two option — and assuming brand matters? I'll assume you'd only find yourself considering this trade-off between a partner and a name-brand fund if you truly felt the gap between the two was on the edge. In this case, I'd prioritize working with the person you trust the most, who is committed to helping you succeed and who you feel will be most aligned with your mission for the duration you need. It's not always the case that investors are equally active in helping you across the entire life cycle of your startup.

One last and very real thing to consider is that partners do move on from funds from time to time, and they don't (generally can't) take their investment in you along with them. So consider the other partners in the fund as part of your selection process as well. Who knows, it might very well be one of them who ends up on your board in the future!

Why are angels important, and how do I choose which angels to have in my round?

Angel investing has increased in popularity over the years because 1) it has become mainstream to invest in startups (thank you, AngelList), and 2) many more alumni (founders and employees) of fast-growing companies have made enough money to help new companies.

These latter types of angels can really help you with your company in the early stages as, not only can they share valuable experience, but they can also make relevant connections that help you with key hires and future raises. As you consider which angels to bring along on your journey, think of your cap table as a roster of skills and connections. Optimize for collecting all the experience you need on your advisory/investment team to take your company to the next level.

Keep in mind, however, that angels don't always have massive investment tickets to write, so that's when it comes in handy to group them with specialized early stage funds that can work alongside them without displacing their value-add as part of an early round. Specialized pre-seed funds can also help manage the mechanics of closing an investment round with many angels and other investors.

9

Managing Your Fundraising Process

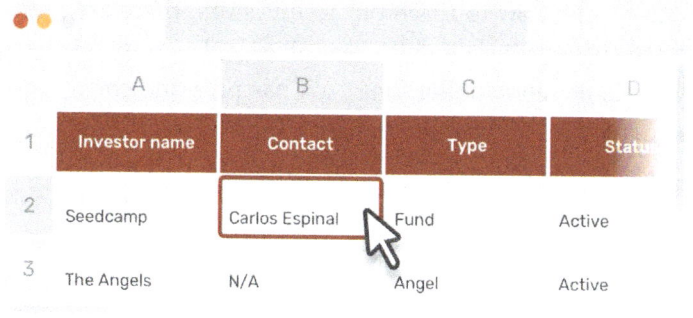

Creating and Managing Your Pipeline

Once you've identified who you want to talk to, organizing the process is simple. Your list for reaching out to investors and managing those relationships is no different than creating a simple sales pipeline (adapted for fundraising of course). In effect, you should have:

1) a list of people you'd like to speak to; 2) a log of how many meetings you've had and how many more you think you need to have until a potential close (more on this later); 3) the probability of the deal closing based on how the conversations went; and 4) next steps for each. Even if you are relying on an entirely inbound and unsolicited process, it's still useful for your decision-making process. The better you manage the process of meeting people, the more effective you will be and the quicker you'll close.

To get a better feel for this process, we'll cover it in more detail in the next section of this chapter, with an example Google Sheet (because it is easier to see/share live changes with others) to help you manage your pipeline.

Regarding how to reach out to investors, there are many strategies out there and it's not always clear which is best. There is no silver bullet, but each has pros and cons. Here are a few (with my names for each):

1. **The One and Only**. You speak to one investor that you like a lot and have a good relationship with because of personal reasons. If you can lock this investor down, that's great for you and you can skip the time-draining process altogether. You should note that this is risky for many founders as it greatly limits their options and makes them reliant on someone else's timeline and willingness to fund.
2. **The Clustered Approach.** Effectively, you start with your top five (no more than 10), see how that goes, whether any are interested, and then move onto the next five, and so forth. Think of this as clusters or waves you go through. That way, you don't dilute your efforts and spread yourself thin by replying to emails from investors

you are less keen on before you have finished meetings with those you prefer. Generally, if the first wave or two fail in creating interest, you should think about continuing your raise at this time. However, if you get early interest, this method has a higher chance of creating momentum for you, and keeping momentum is the most important aspect of driving towards a successful fundraise. You might have received advice on starting with investors that you can practice on, but that sometimes you just causes brand dilution for you (I no longer recommend this unless they are VERY close to you, the market is way too interconnected).

3. **The Spray and Pray.** You contact a large group of investors all at the same time. This can create management issues for you. On the plus side, you have many investors talking about you, which can increase your potential buzz... provided they don't all start rejecting you at the same time, thus accelerating your downfall. Investors will likely second-guess themselves if everyone they know is rejecting you. This strategy works better in a easy-money environment and less so in a cash-constrained environment.

4. **The Social Catchup or the "I'm-Not-Raising" Chat.** Although you should always treat every meeting as a real meeting, a "preview/social chat" meeting differs from a proper fundraising meeting in that it's more of a friendly discussion about your business in the pre-fundraising stage. This lowers the pressure on everyone, but doesn't do away with an investor's tendency to judge you as a founder, your team, and the market size your company operates in. Be mindful that these chats can

still be damaging if you're unprepared for them. These meetings can be great to generate pre-emptive offers though, particularly if you're in a hot investment space or your team comes from a well-known company that is well regarded.

5. **The Stealth Approach.** In the realm of stealth fundraising, a notable shift has occurred since the writing of the first edition of this book. Nowadays, many investors actively use social media sites and company alumni networks to identify potential talent early, often before a startup is even formed. This means that even in stealth mode, there are subtle ways to hint at your interest in raising capital (intentionally or unintentionally). For instance, on LinkedIn, founders might update their profile to indicate they're 'building something new' separate from their past employer, or simply label their current project as a 'stealth company.' The key here is that demonstrating you're involved in a secretive yet intriguing project, especially if you have an impressive background with relevant past experience, can pique investor interest. This stealth approach to fundraising strategy is about subtly signaling your intentions and background, rather than complete concealment.

When considering any of these strategies, keep in mind that competitive dynamics between investors are a really strong source of negotiating power, arguably the best one. With more than one deal on offer, you can better negotiate terms for your investment by leveraging one deal against another, and being able to walk away from a deal you don't like. Keep in mind when I say leveraging, I don't mean signing stuff and backtracking on commitments, what I mean is to have the confidence to negotiate in your favor knowing you have additional investment offers on the table.

However, keep in mind during these discussions that investors talk amongst themselves, even if they are in different/competing firms. Similar to other industries where social events bring you together and you talk shop, it just happens. It happens, either via social events, regular catchups or through established friendships. So be mindful that if you say you have spoken with Bob while you're speaking with Jane, don't be surprised if Jane calls Bob to discuss your company and is swayed positively or negatively by that conversation.

I recommend that you be cautious with your information — keep your cards close to your chest, or at least be selective about what you share and with whom. Ensure there's a strategic purpose behind every piece of information you divulge. This could be to signal your intentions (like an offer you're considering), to outline your desired round composition (such as the syndicate you wish to form or are thinking about), or to indicate the level of interest from other investors. However, it can be advantageous to disclose solid discussions you're having (for example, with reputable investors) to a select few investors whom you're particularly interested in. Sharing this information can sometimes expedite the process for you. Remember, this requires a delicate balance.

Back to reaching out to investors— there are many different ways of doing this. Pick one that works for you and stick with it. For the record, my preference is the Cluster Approach strategy, as it optimizes your time best and can drive momentum if well managed.

Building Your Model Pipeline

In an effort to shed more light on what a potential pipeline could look like, here is a link to a Google Sheet that hopefully you'll find useful in planning your fundraise.

This template will help you focus on who you want to talk to based on the criteria that best suit your company's fundraising needs (e.g. geography, round size, stage, sector focus, etc.) and maximize the connections you have to reach them. While I know people use different tools to track investor comms/relationships, I wanted to offer the below merely as a suggestion for a simplified way to help track and stay on top of the many conversations and relationships needed to aid the fundraising process.

In order to get the most out of this template, consider the following :

1) Copy and paste this template onto a shareable Google Sheet, which you share with your key shareholders and team members that will assist you in reaching the desired connections for your fundraise.

2) In column A, list only names of people who best suit your current fundraise (feel free to create a separate sheet that "archives" people you want to talk to for rounds further down the road).

3) Be disciplined about researching investors' suitability for your raise. Aside from looking at their website, ask other founders or friends/shareholders that have interacted with them to get estimates on all variables, including how much they typically invest, sectors of keen interest and what their

typical fundraising process looks like.

4) Scour your LinkedIn connections and the connections of your key team members and shareholders for the best person(s) within a fund (or angels) to get introduced to.

5) In column G of the template, add the friend/colleague/current investor within your network (as per #4 above) with the strongest relationship to make the introduction to the person you want to meet. If you don't have a direct connection to the person you'd like to talk to, use LinkedIn to identify a connection (a few if possible as not everyone is best friends with people on LinkedIn, and you might need to ask around for the strongest connections) within your network who could help you with an introduction to that person.

6) When the time comes to request an introduction, make it easy on the introducer by drafting a simplified email that they can forward on your behalf which sets out why your opportunity is of interest to the recipient. Attach a one-pager (or more information in a simplified format) about your company so they can get an idea of what you are working on and determine if it's of interest to them. This way, your connection simply has to hit 'forward' with some simple text like "Dear [friend in VC fund], one of my other [friends/investments] would like to talk to you about their raise, more details below, please let me know if of any interest so I can make an intro".

Aside from these steps above, try get your introductions made in a tight time frame and from a diversified set of sources. Nothing is worse than dragging things out longer than you need to or saturating one person with introduction requests (it is less effective anyway). Once you have your list, dedicate a few days to cranking through the introduction requests, sending out emails, replying to first meeting scheduling and getting your fundraise started!

II

Part 2 - Closing Your Investment

"You've got to know when to hold 'em
Know when to fold 'em
Know when to walk away
And know when to run
You never count your money
When you're sittin' at the table
There'll be time enough for countin'
When the dealin's done" – Kenny Rogers

10

Understanding Your Deal

Deal Priorities

In order to get the most out of your investment and investors, you need to focus on what matters most when it comes to your round terms. I've seen many a fundraise derail because initial conversations focused on the wrong things or, worse, missed out on key points simply because others of lesser importance were the focus. Thus, before you engage in conversations with your lead/co-lead investors about deal structures, let's cover a few deal basics you should prioritize:

1. **Focus on the commercial terms of your round first and not the structure.** Focus on how much money you need to build your company and the dilutive impact taking this money would imply. Focus on anything that will affect your current or future growth opportunities first.
2. **Look at your terms comprehensively and what they are trying to achieve.** What are the key things that are necessary for both you and the investor? This includes items like information rights, board rights, etc.
3. **In good times**, numbers 1 and 2 above will likely be quite in line with the 'market' as all investors will be competing. But, **in bad times** and in situations where things are stressful with your company, you might receive terms that indicate a flat or down-round. This is where the deal economics compress your existing shareholders, including the founder's shares. When difficult fundraising times are driven by macro factors (i.e., recessions), you have to factor in the near term impact of receiving funds vs. getting what you'd ideally want. In other words, don't lose sight of the bigger picture (keeping your company

living to fight another day) vs. refusing to factor in the circumstances around your raise and rejecting what might be one of very few offers available.

4. Once you have thought through the above points, **then engage in the conversation about deal structure**. Though, be careful not to fall into the temptation of going for what is popular right now. Founders frequently think they should go with structures that are *en vogue* to close deals, such as a SAFE, convertible, or equity, or whatever. They may have read a blog post with a list of reasons why one is better than the other. My SC colleague Vanessa Vasquez adds: "*When weighing your deal structure options, factors like speed, cost-efficiency, jurisdiction, and valuation should be taken into account. It's important to make decisions based on what aligns best with your specific circumstances, rather than simply following the crowd.*"

5. In some cases, investors may be incentivized to give you more cash if the deal is done in a **specific country or structure** because of tax benefits they may receive (e.g., SEIS in the UK). While this could make things a little trickier for you, it may be worth it for the additional money.

6. Before entering into discussions about deal details with an investor, **decide what you are willing to compromise on to close the deal.** You don't want to dogmatically dismiss some options you might be presented with only to find out that other deals don't materialize — you never know.

7. With all this in mind, **don't get over-complicated or deviate too far from the market norm**. Anything that is new or vastly different in terms of deal structuring will either have unforeseen loopholes at worst or, at

best, additional legal costs from lawyers having to draft something they don't have templates for. Tom McGinn, friend and venture/startup lawyer, adds: "Given that documents are typically rolled forward throughout a company's life cycle, complexity generally leads to more complexity (which can drive up costs/time to complete rounds), so the longer they can keep things simple, the better."

In summary, there are many ways for you and an investor to come to an agreement about structuring to close a round. Don't be hung up on one type of deal structure.

Legal Hour with Tom and Carlos

To go deeper into the above points, during 2020, my colleague Tom Wilson and I recorded a six-episode show called "**Legal Hour with Tom and Carlos**". In it, we set out to cover the core of what this book section covers in much greater detail. The discussion is available in both audio (via podcast) and video (via YouTube).
I highly recommend you give it a listen.

Deal Structures

When you do eventually get to talking about deal structures, you'll be entering into a topic that investors deal with daily —and for most founders, only a handful of times in their company's journey. Deal structures are also always evolving. They can come in all shapes and sizes, ranging from straight-up equity (including ordinary and preferred shares) to convertible notes, warrants, and newer structures such as SAFEs/ASAs/BSA-Airs and "convertible equity" to name a few.

While I won't go into the more exotic variants in depth (plenty of that on the web), below is a quick run-through of some of the more common structures and why they exist. We will then cover equity rounds and convertible notes briefly, as they tend to be the foundation for most commonly used structures in early-stage rounds. In other words, they form the "core" of what other structures offer meaning, other structures are just derivatives of these.

Deal structures tend to fall into one of two categories: 1) **fixed-price structures** and 2) **variable-price structures**

Fixed-Priced Structures - Structures in which the price per share is clearly defined as part of the legal documentation.

- **Ordinary Share Equity Rounds** - Your standard types of rounds, particularly when seeking some sort of tax relief (in the UK via SEIS/EIS).
- **Preferred Share Equity Rounds** - Similar to the above, but involving a new share class with preferred economic rights (e.g., a liquidation preference where investors get their money out first or, anti-dilution rights where, in any subsequent round, there is a non-dilutive effect on shares) over ordinary shares.

Variable Priced Structures - Structures where the price per share is a function of an event or condition at a future date. Thus, while the price per share can be estimated, it will only be fully known at a future date.

- **Convertible Notes** - The OG of variable-priced rounds. We'll go deeper into these below.
- **The Advanced Subscription Agreement (ASA)** was made popular with its use in facilitating SEIS/EIS tax-relief rounds in the UK. Originally, it served as a bridge to a straight-up equity round, but needed to be "converted" relatively soon to make sure it qualified for the tax relief. Since its launch, the conversion timescale to equity to qualify for tax relief has moved forward, thus reducing its original purpose somewhat, but it continues to be popular today. The main technical difference between an ASA and a SAFE (described below), is that ASAs tend to convert on a long stop date while SAFEs don't (because there's no SEIS/EIS-like tax relief structure in the US and therefore no need to convert within a certain period of time).
- **SAFE** - Created by YC in 2013 as a simpler alternative to convertible loan notes, SAFE stands for a Simple Agreement for Future Equity. In Paul Graham's words "We've created a new alternative to convertible notes, called a SAFE.... [They] should work just like convertible notes, but with fewer complications"). In many ways, a SAFE is now the "middle ground" for investment rounds, particularly in the early stages.It has been modified for different jurisdictions. Tom McGinn adds, "Since becoming the default bridge structure in the US, and with the SEIS/EIS conversion period having become shorter in the UK, the SAFE is replacing ASAs as the default in the UK as well."
- **Other variants** - Because it's easy to start with a convertible note and then strip out or add things to it, there are frankly countless varieties of Franken-notes out there that don't have catchy names. Once you understand the concepts that

delineate a fixed-priced structure from a variable one, you will be able to navigate any variety you encounter.

For practical examples of various instruments like convertible loan notes, ASAs, equity round documentation, and more, commonly used in the UK, France, Germany, Portugal, and Denmark, visit Seedsummit.org.

For this book, I chose an average, simple equity round and a convertible note round to break down and explain further. The convertible is the more complex of the variable-priced rounds, so if you understand that, then the SAFE and the ASA will be easier to understand.

Deciphering an Equity Term Sheet

This may seem obvious to some, but to be on the safe side, I want to clarify that when you've received a term sheet for an equity investment, the term sheet is not where the deal ends. Rather, it is merely a summary of the key terms of the deal; more documents will follow before the final deal closes. A typical equity deal can be likened to an iceberg documentation-wise — the tip is merely the term sheet the heavy stuff is under the water.

Another thing to consider when it comes to equity term sheets is that they vary according to jurisdiction. A term sheet that works in the USA or the United Kingdom doesn't necessarily work for a company whose legal headquarters is in Germany. As such, you need to make sure you get legal counsel, particularly if you're not sure about the terms and how they apply to your jurisdiction.

That said, there is a lot of learning you can do to familiarize yourself with the "language" of a typical term sheet. In the US, the Series Seed Documents are the most well known and, as such, it would behoove you to familiarize yourself with them for an early-stage deal based in the US. Seedsummit.org aggregates term sheets that mirror those of the US-centric Series Seed documents, but are repurposed for the UK and certain parts of Europe. Again, review these documents to become familiar with real-life terms. Other resources include the NVCA, BVCA, and EVCA websites, each of which includes links to model documents for different stages.

While I won't go into the legal nitty-gritty of a term sheet, I will quickly summarize the sections so that you can familiarize yourself with the basic structure. A typical term sheet is comprised of several sections that fall into the following buckets:

- **Economics of your deal** (valuation, round size, etc.), including your option pool size.
- **Structure of the deal**, which specifies the type of share (preferred or common/ordinary) as well as any kind of tax relief mechanisms for investors (e.g., SEIS/EIS in the UK).
- **Control provisions**, which investors will want to make sure they feel involved (which control provisions should be included is a topic of much debate). If you want to see some examples, visit VentureBeat.
- **Treatment of a founder's shares if the founder leaves prior to a pre-allotted time**. This is usually done in the form of "reverse vesting", and allows remaining founders to fairly preserve their equity .
- **Board and governance structure**. There are many vari-

ations of an "ideal board," so I won't cover the subject here. However, typically, there is a desire by investors to be involved at the board level in some capacity (again, another topic of debate — particularly whether early-stage investors should have director seats — but, alas, a topic for another day). Generally speaking though, the earlier the stage of the company, the less formality should be expected in the formation of the board, as a board should not burden already time-starved founders with too many meetings and required documentation.
- **Deal fees**. Effectively who will pay for what, in terms of the legals for completion. Typically, the smaller the round, the more likely that each party pays their own legal fees As the rounds get bigger and more costly, it's increasingly more common to have the fees come out of the new fundraising round's capital.
- **Option pool.** Typically, you'll have a clause that shows how much will be allocated to new employees who will be hired after the round closes. One of the best option pool calculators out there right now was created by Index Ventures. It helps you visualize amounts and allocations and I highly recommend it: https://www.indexventures.com/optionplan/#
- **Exclusivity and legal binding**. This is another one of those misunderstood sections. While it is very clear on most term sheets that the document is non-binding (generally the only legally binding part is the exclusivity), it is seen as very bad form to sign a term sheet without the intention of taking the deal once the necessary paperwork (bottom of the iceberg) and due diligence are complete. Naturally, there are always extenuating circumstances, but generally,

it is ill-advised to play games with what you sign.

Deciphering Convertible Notes

Convertible notes and their cousins — SAFEs/ASAs/convertible equity— are different from equity rounds in that they are commercial agreements for a form of *future* equity transaction. What makes them different from each other, is the extent to which they resemble either debt that needs to convert into equity (convertible notes) or a Simple Agreement for Future Equity (SAFEs... literally). In effect, they differ across a spectrum of terms that are either included or excluded because they give investors a mechanism to get paid in absence of a conversion event. If that definition doesn't make sense... don't worry, I'll cover this in more detail shortly. For the sake of simplicity, for the rest of this section, I will focus on convertibles notes because they are the more complex of the variable-priced structures we discussed. The rest of their cousins only get simpler.

I want to share with you an excerpt from an older blog post I wrote on the matter: *"The convertible note (and its derivatives) get lots of attention as an alternative to traditional equity financing; some of this attention is good and some of it is bad. Some investors refuse to use convertible notes, while others love them as a quick way of getting a company the capital it needs."*

Convertible notes are sometimes viewed as a "jack of all trades" from both a company's and an investor's perspective. For the investor, the note is a loan, so they enjoy more downside protection than an equity holder would in the event the company is forced to wind up or dissolve. In other words, the investor enjoys the downside protection typically associated with debt lenders, but is also positioned to enjoy the upside opportunity typically enjoyed by equity holders.

For a company, the upside is: if it eventually raises money by selling shares to later investors in a typical early-stage financing round, then rather than pay back the outstanding amount in cash, the principal and interest are "converted" into shares in the company (usually at a discount to the price offered to new investors—I'll discuss that below).

As with any instrument, it's best to have a thorough understanding of the pros and cons of each of the convertible note's features and how they can be used for your individual circumstances. Fortunately, convertible notes typically have fewer moving pieces than equity instruments do. This explains, in part, why they're sometimes favored by early-stage companies and investors; the negotiation and documentation for a convertible note round are likely to be far less time-consuming and costly than for an equity round. Before we proceed any further, let's look at the basics of a convertible note.

Total amount raised by the note.

This amount does have a natural limit. Think about it this way: you have an amount "outstanding on your cap table" that will be part of an upcoming round. If a new round in the future isn't particularly big, having too much money outstanding can create a problem since your convertible note holders now take up too large a portion of that round. Example: a $1 million convertible that converts as part of a total $2 million seed round would loosely mean that the convertible note holders would have 50 percent of the round. If the round was supposed to be for 20 percent of your equity, that means your new investor will only get 10 percent, an amount that may not excite him that much (more on this in the Toxic Rounds chapter), and you only get 50 percent new money in the door. To limit these extreme cases, investors usually create a "qualified round" definition within the note's conversion terms (see further below), which reduces the likelihood of this amount being disproportionately larger than a new investor's amount as part of a new round.

Discount percentage.

Simply put, if shares are worth $1, a 20 percent discount percentage would mean that a convertible note investor would get the shares for 80 cents. In cases where the next round's valuation is below your convertible note holder's cap (see the next point), a discount factor will yield the convertible note holder equity at a marginally lower price for having taken a risk on you. Typically, this discount percentage is likely to be between 10 and 25 percent. Another example: a round closes at $3 million. Your cap is at $5 million. Your convertible note holders have a 20 percent discount, so they get to convert into the next round at a valuation of $2.4 million.

Limit on company valuation at conversion (the valuation cap).

In order to calculate the number of shares into which the outstanding balance on a convertible note will convert, you must know the price at which the next round's equity securities are being sold. Price per share is calculated by taking the company's pre-money valuation (negotiated at the time of the equity financing between the company and the investors) and dividing that number by the total number of outstanding/issued shares in the company (the company's fully diluted capital) plus anything that can turn into shares (e.g., employee options). Recall, however, that convertible notes are typically entered into in anticipation of an equity financing round. Thus, at the time a convertible note is issued, no one knows what the negotiated pre-money valuation will be if/when the company undertakes equity financing. Consequently, there is no way of knowing what exactly the price per share will be at the time the notes are issued. This creates uncertainty and is a cause of anxiety for some investors, particularly those concerned that the number of shares into which their note may convert may be insignificant relative to the other shareholders, particularly if the pre-money valuation at the time of conversion is especially high. The valuation cap is intended to ease investor concerns by placing a maximum pre-money (or increasingly, post-money, as it's easier to calculate) valuation on the company at the time of conversion. With a cap, an investor effectively sets the minimum amount of equity they require for participating in your convertible note round. For example, if you have a $200,000 note on a valuation with a $5 million cap, the worst-case scenario for the convertible note holder would be 4 percent equity (0.2/5 = 4 percent) after the new round is over. In effect, the further north the valuation cap is from what you expect your pre-money valuation to be for your next round, the less you should care about the cap, since it is less likely to affect you negatively.

The rising prevalence of uncapped notes.

This may seem like a founder-friendly outcome which is nice to get if possible, but it can have negative outcomes if too much is raised on uncapped structures. Even if structured well, an uncapped note can make an investor feel "unprotected" should the company do exceedingly well and their note converts into a much smaller equity percentage than originally hoped, reducing the number of investors interested in uncapped structures. So, if you as the founder suggest it, you may not receive it, particularly in non-competitive scenarios.

The interest rate on a note.

A convertible note is a form of debt, or loan. As such, it usually accumulates interest, typically 4-8 percent from the point when you sign it to when it converts. These days, the interest accrual usually converts into equity as part of the overall amount at the next round. For example, if your loan note is $100 with an annual interest rate of 8 percent, then you'd convert $108 into equity after a year. An interest rate is still seen on some convertible notes but is increasingly less common because times have changed and the taking interest on an investment is no longer preferred as it erodes working capital. Note: in the US, it's highly advisable to include an interest rate (if you use this particular type of structure over a SAFE), even if it's simply a nominal amount equal to the applicable federal rate. If you don't include an interest rate, any amount that could have been earned via interest is taxed to the company as a gain. So it's not really an option to exclude it in the US. In the UK, you don't necessarily need to include an interest rate should you wish to omit it.

Conversion events & triggers.

The point of a convertible note is for it to convert at some point in the future, not for it to stay outstanding indefinitely. As such, the note will likely specify a series of conversion triggers. One I mentioned earlier is the next "qualified round". Basically, this means that the round is both big enough to accommodate the amount in the note (without preventing new investors from reaching their ownership targets) and give the note holders the types of rights they'd expect for their shares once converted from loan to equity. Tom McGinn adds: *"Another reason why investors may want a Qualified Round concept is just to ensure that the note converts as part of a legitimate round, particularly if there's no valuation cap (in other words, e.g. avoid the note converting at something silly like a $50K round at a $50m pre-money valuation)."* Another conversion trigger is an expiration maturity date, on which the note holder typically can either ask for their money back (although this rarely happens) or basically seek to convert the outstanding amount at that point. Upon a change-of-control event in the future, and before the convertible is converted, investors can sometimes ask for a multiple of their loan back as payment in lieu of converting to ordinary shares prior to the completion of the change-of-control event. There are more types of conversion triggers that note makers can add to a note, but these are the basic ones.

These are the headline terms of a convertible note and are not representative of all possible terms. However, for early discussions with potential investors, you'll rarely talk about anything more than the items above. Beyond that, you'll likely have to involve lawyers (or experienced deal drafters) to help you finalize the document. Also keep in mind that realistically, investors will never treat this as a proper debt instrument, even if it resembles one, as expectations will be that it's in lieu of an equity round. However, always keep in mind that it only takes one investor to have the wrong expectation to create problems!

Now let's recap the pros and cons of using a convertible note.

Pros

- Typically less complicated and therefore require less paperwork than equity rounds (because you're effectively deferring the investment terms discussion to a later round).They can cut down on legal fees and the time to get money.
- Investors enjoy downside protection as debt holders during the earliest and critical growth stages of the company.
- At conversion, note holders typically receive discounts or valuation caps on the converting balance, thereby rewarding the earliest investors appropriately without causing valuation issues.
- Convertibles notes can defer the negotiations surrounding valuation until later in your company's life cycle (i.e., for companies at the earliest stages of planning and prepara-

tion, valuations can be more difficult to define).

Cons

- If a convertible note is too large, it can negatively impact your next round because it will convert to a disproportionately large portion of that round (toxic round), effectively crowding out your next round's potential investors from having the equity stake they may desire.
- If a convertible note's cap is too low, the founders may need to take the additional dilution that would happen if they exceeded the convertible's cap in order to accommodate a larger round later.
- Because a convertible note can be quite versatile, investors can add clauses that have greater implications down the road, such as being able to take up more of a future round than the actual amount they've put in. Tom McGinn adds: "*MFNs are fairly standard (which effectively make it harder to do another bridge on better terms prior to conversion)."* From Thomson Reuters Practical Law, an MFN is: "*Business jargon for the concept that the first party will be entitled to at least as favorable terms as a second party in specified circumstances.* "
- If not careful, you can accumulate too much convertible debt, which may burden you at a conversion point. To explore why in more detail, check out this article that covers it in detail: https://techcrunch.com/2017/07/08/why-safe-notes-are-not-safe-for-entrepreneurs/
- Doesn't give your investors SEIS tax relief (in the UK), thus making it less attractive than an equity round.
- Convertible note holders receive the same investor rights

as future investors. If the future round includes preferred shares, this may confer more rights than what an equity investor would have received had they simply done an equity deal on ordinary shares with you.
- If the convertible note automatically converts at the next equity raise, investors may wind up being forced to convert into shares, despite not being happy with the terms of the equity financing. The note holders may unfortunately have less influence in negotiating the terms of the equity financing, which partially explains why some investors are reluctant to invest with convertible notes.
- Finally, while convertible notes allow the company to defer the valuation conversation until a later time, any inclusion of a conversion cap will raise a similar conversation, which defeats some of the purpose of the convertible note being a quick-and-easy financing solution to begin with.

Now let's explore a few more core concepts attributable to convertible notes that are neither strictly a pro or con, but unique attributes about the structure:

Seniority. A convertible note is a form of debt or loan. Although it's not too common to hear about investors asking for their money back, they in fact do have that right. Additionally, one of the privileges of having the note act as a form of debt is that it acts senior to equity in the case of a liquidation. What this means in practice is that note holders will get their money back first.

Subscription Rights. Some investors like to have more equity than their invested amount would likely yield them upon conversion. As a result, one thing to look out for is how much they want to take up of the next round as part of having been in the convertible note. To add some color to this, here's an example: an investor gives you $500,000, which converts at your next round of some large-ish valuation. This might yield that investor next to nothing in terms of equity percentage ownership. However, that investor had a subscription right for up to 20 percent of the new round, so that allows them to participate on the new round with more money, thus affording them a larger "seat at the table" in excess of the small percentage he would have had without this right.

Cap Tables

To provide you with some practical examples on how equity rounds and convertible rounds impact your cap table, my colleague Felix Martinez and I have created a small series of YouTube clips that illustrates how both affect your cap table. I highly recommend you check them out as they go through the theory and the application of the theory. Simply go to Seedcamp's Youtube Channel:
https://www.youtube.com/c/seedcamp/videos

Syndicates and Best Practices

Whether you raise your money via an equity round, convertible or other deal structure, you'll likely have a few investors gather together to raise the total amount you desire. This gathering is called a syndicate — a fancy term for the various investors who come together to form your investment round.

Before we get started, let's look at a few handy definitions:

- **Lead Investor**. Usually sets the terms, and deals with managing the flow of communications among investors.
- **Co-Leads**. Two (or more) investors who decide to equally split the work of lead investor, usually taking the same amount of equity for cash.
- **Follow(on) Investor(s)**. Usually in the round on whatever terms are set by the lead investor(s).

Generally speaking, a good lead investor will, as the name implies, lead the communication and negotiation of the terms among all parties within the syndicate. This is where having a good lawyer can significantly help you in terms of managing the legal process, which I'll cover in a later section. In some cases, particularly if you see that communications are not going well between all parties, you will need to step in and lead. You should be involved in all cases anyway, but just keep an eye out to see if the lead investor is managing the process well. If they aren't, other investors will usually complain. Even if your lead is doing a good job, you will likely have to manage various people's questions and expectations about the timing of a round's close and other concerns. Sometimes people just want to talk to you!

Negotiations

Pick your battles!

Negotiation is a bit of a weird subject because your strategy is very relative to your negotiation power. In situations where you have only one offer, very limited cash runway, and a huge gap between what you wanted and what you got offered, your ability to get "the perfect offer" will be quite low. On the other end of the spectrum, if you have competing term sheets, you have a better chance of relying on one to negotiate the other, since you can walk away from at least one deal, and if you're in a hyper-competitive situation, you likely can even go as far as setting the terms you want (within reason)!

Assuming you will have some negotiations, however, the best thing you can do to improve your chances of closing a round on the terms you want is to create competitive dynamics between interested parties.

Regardless of the number of offers in hand, eventually you will find yourself in the process of actually going through the points you want to negotiate. The first thing I recommend is to take a step back and look at the overall offer.

- Is it very far away from what you expected?
- If so, what does this say about your investor?
- Is she giving you economics that imply she doesn't think you're far along enough, or perhaps your valuation is misaligned?
- Is she giving you an offer that includes heavier-than-normal governance?

If these kinds of questions come up, consider having a conversation about them before making a counter-offer. It is very easy to get carried away with wanting to negotiate away everything you think is unfair about a prospective deal, but you run the risk of making it unlikely to close at all. By turning your concerns into a conversation, and a level-headed one at that, you have a higher likelihood of coming to an amicable agreement that comes closer to each party's interests.

11

Understanding Valuation

One of the most frequently asked questions at any startup event or investor panel is: **how do investors value a startup?** The unfortunate answer is: it depends largely on the market we are operating in at the time you are fundraising.

As frustrating as it may be, startup valuation is a relative science, not an exact one.

The biggest determinants of your startup's value are the

market forces of the industry and sector it plays in, (including the balance or imbalance between demand and supply of money), the size and recent occurrence of comparable company exits, the willingness for an investor to pay a premium to get into a deal, and the level of desperation of the entrepreneur looking for money.

While the above may capture the bulk of how most early-stage startups are valued, I appreciate that it lacks the specificity you're looking for, so the details of valuation methods will be explored next in the hope of shedding some light on how you can determine the value of your startup.

As any newly minted MBA graduate will tell you, there are many valuation tools and methods out there. They range in purpose from valuing small companies to large, and vary in the number of assumptions you need to make about a company's future relative to its past performance to get a "meaningful" valuation. Knowing which method is the best to use for your circumstance is just as important as knowing how to use these tools in the first place.

Some of the valuation methods you may have heard of include:

- The DCF (Discounted Cash Flow[10]).
- The First Chicago Method[11].
- Market & Transaction Comparables[12].
- Asset-based valuations such as the Book Value[13] or the

---

[10] https://en.wikipedia.org/wiki/Discounted_cash_flo

[11] https://en.wikipedia.org/wiki/First_Chicago_Metho

[12] https://en.wikipedia.org/wiki/Comparable_transaction

[13] https://en.wikipedia.org/wiki/Book_valu

Liquidation Value[14].

While going into the details of how these methods work is outside the scope of this book (and irrelevant for early-stage startups), we can start tackling the issue of valuation by investigating what investors look for and which methods provide the best proxy for current value.

Market Dynamics

A startup's value today is largely dictated by the market forces in the industry in which it operates and today's perception of what the future will bring (where the present value calculation comes from).

On the downside, this means that if your company is operating in a space where your market or industry is depressed and the outlook for the future isn't any good, then clearly what an investor is willing to pay for the company's equity is going to be substantially reduced, even though your company may already be successful. Though, there are exceptions when the investor is privy to information about a potential market shift in the future, or is just willing to take the risk that the company will be able to shift the market. (I will explore the latter point on what can influence your attainment of a better or worse valuation in greater detail later.) Obviously, if your company is in a hot market, the inverse will be the case.

Therefore, when an early-stage investor is trying to determine whether to invest in a company (and what the appropriate valuation should be), they basically gauge what the likely exit

---

[14] https://en.wikipedia.org/wiki/Liquidation_valu

size will be of a company of your type within the industry in which it plays. They then will judge how much equity their fund should have in the company to reach their return on investment goals, relative to the amount of money put into the company throughout its lifetime.

This may sound quite hard for investors to do considering they don't know how long it will take the company to exit, how many rounds of cash it will need, and how much equity the founders will let them have in order to meet their goals. However, through the variety of deals they hear about and see in seed, they have a mental picture of what constitutes "average" for the size of a round, price and the amount of money your company will raise relative to others in the same space. In addition to having a pulse of what is going on in the market, VCs effectively have financial models that make assumptions about what will likely happen to a company they are considering for investment. Based on these assumptions, investors will decide how much equity they effectively need now, knowing that they may have to invest along the way (if they can) so that when your company reaches the point of going to an exit, they will hit their return on investment goal. If they can't make the numbers work for an investment in terms of what a founder is asking for or what the markets are telling them via their assumptions, an investor will either pass, or wait around to see what happens (if they can).

The next logical question is: **how does an investor size the "likely" maximum value (at exit) of my company in order to do their calculations?**

There are several methods investors use to arrive at this number, all of which are either "instinctual" or quantitative. Instinct is used more in early-stage deals. As the company grows and matures, its financial information along with quantitative methods are increasingly applicable. Instinctual analyses are not entirely devoid of quantitative considerations, however—it's just that these methods of valuation are driven mostly by an investor's sector experience of average deals at entry and exit. The quantitative methods are not that different, they just incorporate more figures to extrapolate a series of potential exit scenarios for your company. For quantitative-heavy calculations, the market and transaction comparables method is the favored approach. Comparables tell an investor how other companies in the market are being valued — which in turn can be applied to your company as a proxy for your value today. This is why, in a market where there are more and more privately funded companies with billion dollar valuations (and/or acquisitions), you see an effective rise in valuations overall (and if those valuations get corrected in a downturn, then it also affects the entire market).

Most valuation tools include a market influence factor, meaning a part of the calculation is determined by how the market is doing, be it the market/industry your company operates in, or the larger S&P 500 stock index. This makes it hard to use tools (such as the DCF) that try and use a startup's past performance as a means by which to extrapolate future performance. Comparables— particularly transaction comparables—are favored for early-stage startups, as they are better indicators of what the market is willing to pay for startups similar to the one an investor is considering.

How Does an Estimated Exit Value for Your Company Lead to a Valuation?

Again, knowing what the exit price will be, or having an idea of what it will be, means that a calculation-minded investor can calculate what their returns will be on any valuation relative to the amount of money they put in, or alternatively, what their equity percentage will be in an exit (money they put in / the post-money valuation of your company = their percentage).

Before we proceed, just a quick review of some terms:

- Pre-money = the value of your company now.
- Post-money = the value of your company after the investors put the money in.
- Cash-on-Cash Multiple = the multiple of money returned to an investor on exit, divided by the amount they put in throughout the lifetime of the company.

If an investor knows what percentage they own after they invest, and they can guess the exit value of your company (and their return by multiplying % ownership with estimated exit-value); to do so they can divide the exit value to them by the cash invested and get a cash-on-cash multiple of their investment (ideally this is 10x or greater). *For example: They invest 1.5M for 20% of your company, they then get diluted down to 10% over the lifetime of their investment even after putting in an additional 750K of follow-on funding, your company exits at 500M, thus 10% of 500M is 50M, and divided by the 2.25M they invested, nets the investor a 22X on their invested capital.* Some investors use IRR values as well of course, but most investors tend to think in terms of cash-on-cash returns because of the nature of how

VC funds work (which is they have to clear a certain threshold of returned capital they are given by their investors before they have personal returns, known as 'Carry').

Assuming a 10x+ multiple for cash-on-cash returns is what every investor wants from an early-stage venture deal, we'll use that as an example. Keep in mind, this is an incomplete demonstration as there is no requirement for a follow-on investment and investors know this is a rare case when they invest. As such, investors need to incorporate assumptions about how much more money your company will require, and thus how much dilution they (and you) will take provided they do (or don't) follow their money up to a point. Note that not every investor can follow on in every round until the very end, as they often reach the maximum investment amount determined by their fund structure.

Now, armed with assumptions about the value of your company at exit, how much money it may require along the way, and what the founding team (and current investors) may be willing to accept in terms of dilution, an investor will determine a range of acceptable valuations (or equity-stake ranges) that will allow them to meet their returns expectations (or not, in which case they will pass on the investment for "economic" reasons). I call this method the top-down approach.

Naturally, if there is a top-down, there must be a bottom-up as well. While it's based on the top-down assumptions, the bottom-up approach basically takes the average entry valuation (or percentage equity taken for cash) for companies of a certain type and stage an investor typically sees, and values a company relative to that entry average. The entry average used by the bottom-up approach is based on a figure that will likely give investors a meaningful return on an exit for the industry in question. This valuation method might lead an investor to respond to your term sheet like this: "A company of your stage will probably require X millions to grow for the next eighteen months, and therefore based on your current stage, you are worth the following pre-money = [(money you are raising) divided by (total percent ownership the investor wants after the round closes)—(money you are raising)]".

One of the best ways to visualize the bottom-up approach is to read the *Fortune.com* article titled "Behind the VC Numbers[15]". Here you can see what the typical ranges are that investors are taking and, as a consequence, how your numbers will align (or not) with what's expected. Although the article was penned in 2013 (ancient history it feels now!) and will naturally age as a reference point, it does a great job of highlighting how market conditions affect an investor's tolerance for risk (and their reaction in terms of what they request equity-wise to compensate).

Now that we've established how much the market and industry in which your company plays can dictate its ultimate value, let's look at what other factors can cause an investor to either ask for a discount in value or, pay a premium over the average entry price for your company's stage and sector.

An investor is willing to pay more for your company if:

- **It is in a sector that is hot right now.**
- **Your management team is exceptional.** Serial entrepreneurs can command a better valuation. A good

---

[15] http://fortune.com/2013/10/17/behind-the-vc-numbers-higher-prices-less-control

team gives investors faith that you can execute.
- **You have a functioning product**.
- **You have traction**. Nothing shows value like customers telling the investor you have value.
- **You have created a competitive dynamic between investors during your fundraise.**

An investor is less likely to pay a premium over the average for your company (or may even pass on the investment) if:

- **It is in a sector that has shown poor performance.**
- **It is in a sector that is highly commoditized**, with slim margins
- **It is in a sector that has a large set of competitors** with little differentiation among them.
- **Your management team has no track record** and/or may be missing key people for you to execute the plan (and you have no one lined up).
- **Your product is not working** and/or you have no customer validation.
- **You are going to shortly run out of cash**.

In summary, market forces right now, today, greatly affect the value of your company. Investors will consider where similar deals are being priced (bottom-up) and the amount of recent exits (top-down), both of which can affect the value of a company in your specific sector. The best thing you can do is to arm yourself with a feeling for the values in the market before you speak to an investor by speaking to other startups like yours (effectively making your own mental comparables table) that have raised money. See if they'll share with you what valuation they were given and how much they raised at your stage. Additionally, stay current on tech news, which will occasionally give you the information you need to backtrack valuations. Remember, nothing increases your company's value more than showing an investor that people out there want your product and are even willing to pay for it.

As a final thought, if you feel bullish about your ability to raise capital (as in, you have leverage over investors in raising capital because your business is trending) and you have early investor interest, it will always be better for you to agree (if you can) on a fixed equity percentage with your lead investor, rather than a fixed valuation. The reason is simple: by agreeing to a fixed percentage, you can easily increase the size of cash in your round with no additional dilutive effect. If you agree to a fixed valuation as a starting point, with every additional dollar you take, you will be increasing the dilutive effect of the round, thus reducing your incentive to raise more capital if the opportunity to do so presents itself. However, keep in mind that in a market/industry that is dense with competitors fighting for the same market, regardless of whether you can achieve a fixed percentage with a lead investor, it might still benefit you to take as much capital as you can, as your competitors are likely doing the same.

Valuation Discrepancies Around the World

There's one more issue to address regarding valuation: **why are there valuation discrepancies for comparable companies across the world (more specifically at the investment stage rather than the exit stage)?**

The answer has to do with liquidity of deals, the localized

risks for investors, and the supply of investors.

As you just learned, various factors play into how an investor values a startup, but using market comparables from deals done in the US doesn't always incorporate all the risks that are prevalent in the specific geography where the company and investor in question operate. Furthermore, the availability of capital in any given geography will also affect how an investor gauges their own risk/reward ratio when pricing deals.

I'm going to talk about this point abstractly and without incorporating the argument of the global nature of internet-based businesses (they do have some localization risk still, but less so). So, for example, startup exits for investors in certain developing economies will happen less often than, say, in Silicon Valley. This has to do not only with the number of companies coming out of those countries, but also with the universe of potential buyers for these companies in that geography.

This affects the risk an investor takes, as he is less likely to get the 10x return discussed previously. Therefore, the investor will seek a "discount" to take on a deal in order to have a portfolio of deals wherein there is the possibility of exiting in spite of whatever market conditions exist locally. Add to that the fact that the investor may be one of very few investors (short supply of capital), and therefore can command a discount more forcefully than if more competition existed. (Once enough investors exist, market pricing becomes more stable and in parity with other larger markets.)

Maximizing your Valuation

In the previous section, I covered how several factors about your company can influence what valuation you might be able to achieve, including its macro and geographic contexts, among several other factors. Further, the previous section also addressed how traditional finance-driven valuation methods (DCF, etc.) were inappropriate for early-stage startups, even if some of the elements that drive those finance-driven valuation methods were still applicable, such as expected revenues. Let's revisit those points.

The key drivers for maximizing your valuation are:

1. **Excellent metrics.** As different types of businesses have different types of metrics, the general point here is that numbers talk and... Well, you know how that expression goes. Do your numbers show strong customer interest? Do they show a sustainable business? Do your numbers show your ability to bring in cash (within the time frame that's expected of your industry)?
2. **Excellent ability to generate FOMO.** What generates FOMO is hard to pin down, but can usually be traced back to elements that the founding team has, which when combined with the problem they are tackling, creates plausible "magic". While I believe most people intrinsically have the ability to create FOMO, there is an art-form to understanding how others will perceive what you are working on and generating an honest trust in you and your team, rather than relying on simple theatrics to try and achieve the same effect.
3. **The size of your raise.** The bigger the raise, the higher

the valuation needed to avoid washing out the existing shareholders.

The following two are equally important to consider timing-wise, but less within your control to effect:

1. **Positive macro-economic sentiment and confidence.** These externalities influence whether investors will pay higher valuations now. In a down market, the opposite happens, investors get slower and more reluctant to invest.
2. **Sector "hotness."** In effect, this drives investor demand for what you do: the higher the demand, the higher the valuation. In 2017 and 2021, the crypto craze drove hotness.As of writing in 2023, the AI craze for sure is an example of a sector where investors are almost price insensitive!

As I've written on metrics and FOMO before, I want to focus on the last three points for this chapter.

In previous chapters I touched upon the basic fundraising equation:

[Money Raised / Post Money = % Dilution] or alternatively [Money Raised / % Dilution = Post Money], where "valuation" is typically used interchangeably with "pre-money valuation", which is equal to [Post Money — the Money Raised].

The key element to consider with the above equation is that it's not static. The variables that make up the equation change with time. These changes create high and low ranges that are acceptable for investors and founders. We'll cover how those come into play in more detail below.

As covered before, it all starts with macro-economic conditions and general sentiment in public markets. When things are going well, all companies rise—a country's stock index rises, valuations rise, and the tolerance of buyers and investors to invest more and at higher valuations also rises. With all of that on the rise, at the earlier stages, this manifests itself by investors being able to tolerate increasingly more "expensive" rounds—as in, rounds where they have to pay a higher valuation—because they see a possibility of selling their share of the company at a higher valuation in the future.

Again, the first point is that, in good times, investors are willing to increase post-money valuations. In bad times, this will no longer be the case, and if you want to read more on how to brace for that, I've covered it in more detail in the Appendix on weathering bad times.

Another important point is that the more mature the ecosystem, the more capital there is at play. As well as a greater volume of money, there will be more specialized and sophisticated investors who can better judge the potential of your company and may, therefore, pay more. The more investors and money around the table, the more competitive deals get, which will affect your valuation for the better. This is why it is easier to raise money at a higher valuation in California versus an emerging ecosystem.

These two points above imply that there is no "static" view of valuation. Rather, it's dynamic, because of how affected they are by externalities.

Think Ranges

While you'd never share this detail with a prospective investors, internally, it's more constructive to think of valuations as being within an "acceptable" or "probable" range relative to the amount of capital you are raising. This range has an upper and lower boundary, which bookend what your valuation could be. From an investor's point of view:

The UPPER percentage dilution boundary — No early-stage investor is looking to take a majority stake in your business as that would likely constitute an acquisition, so you can easily remove taking 50 percent of your company at a round from the table. Therefore, your "real" upper boundary is usually imposed on the investor by a few factors out of their control, including the competitiveness of the local ecosystem, the options of capital available to you as a founder, and how much the investor cares about how they could be perceived by other investors (some investors don't care if they come across as predatory).

The LOWER percentage dilution boundary — No early-stage investor is likely to give you money for free. As investors compete for your deal, they will be keen on offering you more money for less dilution to you, but there is a limit. As investors calculate what is the minimum they need to return a positive investment to their investors (based on macro conditions and expectations of the future of your company), there is a point where they simply can't make the numbers work as they need them to and they opt out of offering you a deal. Often, this can occur if an alternative offer from an investor at a higher valuation (lower dilution) comes into play that you, as a founder, are considering. Investors who understand your industry better will naturally have more tolerance towards higher valuations (i.e.,. lower percentage dilution) as they can see the future potential of the company more clearly.

Inspired by some of the analysis Kirsty Nathoo from YC has done on the subject, my colleague in SC's Legal Team, Guisela Figueredo adds: *"In a tight market, when founders are raising money on post-money convertibles, it's important for them to maintain a level-headed approach to the "high valuation hype" and aim for a reasonable valuation which considers the realistic potential valuation at which they could raise the subsequent equity round (conversion event). This is because the convertible investors will convert at the lower of the cap price and the equity round price. This in turn means that the expected founders' dilution calculated from round size/valuation cap is a floor, not a ceiling. In other words, if you raise money at a $50M cap on the post-money convertible but then you agree on a $20M pre-money cap in the equity round, the convertible investors will end up with a larger ownership percentage than initially anticipated"*

From a founder's point of view, therefore, you want to push toward a lower percentage dilution boundary through the variables you can control, metrics, FOMO, and round size (more to cover later).

Even though the boundaries above seem like they provide an endless amount of options, it actually sets the stage for a way of thinking of your company's value—as a range of options relative to the amount of capital you are raising, instead of as a fixed value.

So what's an acceptable range then? Well, if the range is dictated by macro conditions, then surely there is some sort of rule of thumb? Luckily there is, but it's confusing as it's different for angels versus institutional investors, and with new types of investors coming online (e.g., pre-seed investors), that just adds more to the mix. However, there is still a "range" that you can use.

SeedLegals (a Seedcamp company) compiled some statistics around valuations for pre-seed and seed rounds in the UK, for example, and this is the range they found (note: the y-axis is 'volume' of funding rounds they have observed):

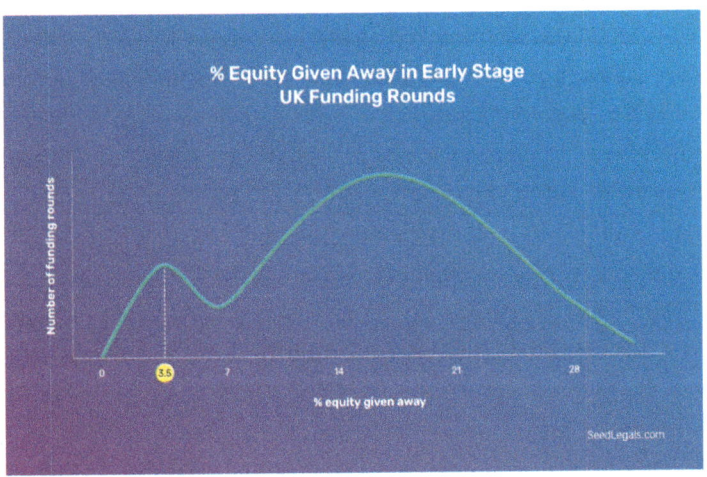

If you zoom out, you see the main curve is between 12% and 25% (my interpretation of the 3.5% blip in the data is the volume of deals that are friends/family). To put that in context, if you were raising a $1 million seed round, that would be the difference between a $4 million post-money valuation (1m /25%) and a $8.3 (1m/12%) million valuation. Yes, it may seem like 4-8m is a wide range, but it also helps provide you with a workable range, and helps you contextualize what might be possible within "the norm" (excluding crazy metrics or FOMO).

However, as mentioned in the 5th point above (on the size of your raise), round size affects your valuation . As you can see, if I take the same range of dilution of 12 percent to 25 percent, then a $2 million round would generate a post-money valuation range of $8 million to $16.6 million. Quite the jump right? Simply put, though you can't control the macro factors that determine the range you operate in, as a founder, you have total control over your round size, which is your primary tool in changing your valuation —along with showcasing strong metrics and developing the factors that can generate FOMO for your industry.

But it's not simply about increasing your round size to extract the valuation range you want —you will be evaluated based on what you've achieved and how you will effectively use the funds raised. So, there is a point where investors may very well think you're raising too much for where you are, and that will be up to the discretion of the investor relative to your industry (and the implied valuation that that amount of cash will imply for them—more on that below).

***Extra geek math on how to find a round size range based on the above**—If you want to figure out what a probable round size for your company could be, mapped with the percent dilution range from SeedLegals as a starting point, you could backsolve for what acceptable ranges might be for you. For example, pick a valuation, assume it represents the pre-money and solve for your round-size, assuming the range of between 25 percent and 12 percent as per their graph. You will end up with a viable round size of your raise* *based on averages as per the data. Can you do better than that? For sure, but now you know how to calculate it!*

In conclusion, you can't control macro-economic conditions nor can you control how upper and lower boundaries change over time for investors, but you can control how much you are raising, and that affects your valuation just as much.

So What's Your Valuation?

OK, so now that you have clarity on how all of this works, and how much you want to raise, you might be wondering: "So what do I say to a lead investor who asks me what my valuation is?"

This is where it gets tricky, because even if you think you know what all the numbers should be, you can either be bold and set a valuation that's as high as you want it and run the risk of pricing yourself out of the market relative to what investors might be interested in at your stage. Or you run the risk of giving a number that's too low only to egret it later.

The good thing is that part of negotiating a valuation is understanding how within-or-outside of the norm your expectations are. Now that you are armed with the math from this section, that should no longer be a mystery for you. Besides offering up a valuation, your other alternative is to offer an understanding of what the market might be for what you are raising. In my colleague Tom Wilson's words, you can say *"We're raising an X-sized round and we expect to dilute a usual amount for this stage. We're really excited about a number of the conversations we're having and what the pricing comes out as a function of that. We're also not necessarily optimizing for the highest price but rather the investor that we think is the best fit for us."*

What's important to take away from the above is that you say you know what the market is and that you acknowledge the investor might have a view, but that you will have a view too. Furthermore, it also showcases you are likely optimizing for what matters (as per the chapter on choosing your investor), over simply optimizing for a valuation.

12

Toxic Rounds

What Do The Following Company Circumstances Have in Common?

(Note: all these examples are anonymized, real, early-stage company experiences.)

- A founder who gave away **> 60 percent of his company** for $100,000 in tranched funding.
- A founder who gave away **> 75 percent of his company** to his "investors" in a pre-Series A round.
- A company that gave away **> 40 percent of its equity** for < $100,000 to investors, but still wanted to go through an accelerator.
- Another company with **51 percent of the company owned by existing investors.**
- Another company where the founder **took five rounds of investment but all in outstanding convertible notes (and/or SAFEs, ASAs**, etc) and not yet converted.
- Another company where the investor offered the founders a sub-$30,000 investment but it **came in as tranches across the year (as in no cash up-front)**.

These circumstances might seem very normal to you, or you might be reeling in shock. Either way, I want to highlight the concept of a toxic round or a toxic cap table in an early-stage startup to help founders navigate potential investment offers and avoid getting themselves into a difficult situation in the future.

What Is a Toxic Round?

A **"Toxic round"** is my non-technical term for a fundraising round that can predispose a company to struggle to find subsequent financing because newer investors shy away from a potential investment once they discover the state of the company's current cap table and/or governance.

Each company's financing history is unique so it is hard to make any judgments about the quality of investors. However, the common view is that investors who ask for terms such as those highlighted in the anecdotes above **are usually not of the sort one wants to take investment from**. My focus here isn't to highlight the qualities of ideal investors, as I covered that already (and if you want to read more about that, check out this text[16]), but rather, to discuss how these kinds of rounds can cause subsequent new investors to shy away from investing in your company. Also, note that I will only focus on founder dilution and not on other potential aspects of a company's shareholdership that could make it difficult for new investors to invest (such as having investors that are not a good fit for your new investors to work with).

New investors may avoid companies that have experienced a toxic round because:

1. The company will likely require more capital in the future should it prove successful, so potential investors feel that **the founders will be less motivated to stick with the**

---

[16] http://www.seedcamp.com/resources/what-tier-is-your-investor-or-what-to-look-for-in-an-investo

company as the value of their equity declines over time through premature excessive dilution.
2. They feel that **current investors own too much of the company** which could create governance issues.
3. The investors have a large stake, which brings up a lot of questions about **how the company got itself into that situation**. Was it through a down-round? Or were there other negative circumstances that could affect the future of a new investment?
4. They may object to their investment being used for **anything other than expanding the growth of a company**. Existing investors eager to dump their shares as part of the financing transaction or companies that have too much debt outstanding repayable as part of an upcoming round will be unattractive to new investors.

With all this in mind, how can we more precisely define a toxic round? Well, a toxic round is one in which either "too much money" comes in too early at too low a valuation, or a company is too under-valued, or both. Both cases lead to founders being excessively diluted too early in their company's life.

To help you calculate these potential scenarios, let's look at these by-now familiar equations as they apply to equity rounds (*convertible structures can have much more complicated variations on dilution outcomes on conversion, particularly if you have several of them outstanding... a possible sign of possible dangers ahead*):

- Money Raised / Post-Money = percent dilution to founders
- Money Raised / (Pre-Money + Money Raised) = percent owned by the new investors

These two equations represent the same thing; the only things that change are the definitions, but the numbers are all the same.

Knowing the above, it would seem the way to avoid a toxic round would be to **raise the right amount of money (helpful with milestones) and set the right valuation for the company early on.** As mentioned before, there are many methods one can take to arguably "price" a company. However, the larger point is that no matter what quantitative method you use, your valuation will always be subject to current market dynamics. **If you are in a boom, the pricing will likely be higher; if you are in a bust, it will likely be lower.** It's as simple as that.

To help you visualize the above calculations in today's market, Jasenko Hadzic from Backingminds.com wrote an interesting LinkedIn post on the subject of broken cap tables, aka toxic rounds that broke the cap table, and came up with this illustration that gives a pretty accurate representation of what equity ownership makes sense at what stage of your company to avoid being tarnished for future rounds.

How does a "broken cap table" look like?

		Founder holdings post-round (+/- 5%)								
	Cap table scenarios	Idea	Pre-seed	Pre-seed	Seed	Seed	Series A	Series B	Series C	Series D	Series E
Founder Holdings	Best-case cap table	100%	90%	80%	70%	60%	50%	40%	30%	20%	10%
	Acceptable cap table	90%	80%	70%	60%	50%	40%	30%	20%	10%	
	Tricky cap table	80%	70%	60%	50%	40%	30%	20%	10%		
	Broken Cap table	70%	60%	50%	40%	30%	20%	10%			
		60%	50%	40%	30%	20%	10%				
		50%	40%	30%	20%	10%					
		40%	30%	20%	10%						
		30%	20%	10%							
		20%	10%								

BackingMinds

All of this begs the question: what if you're already in a tricky situation similar to the examples I noted above or as per the above chart?

There can be many creative solutions to solving the problem with your investors, such as investors giving back equity if founders hit certain milestones However, available solutions aren't always easy and straightforward; in fact, the single best solution is to have a tough talk with existing investors about how to rectify the situation before new investors either walk away or make it conditional as part of their new investment. Most solutions will seem "creative" to a new investor rather than "clean" if not completed before they invest. So, **work through toxicity with existing investors** and help them understand that by not helping you overcome the situation, they may very well be jeopardizing the long-term value of their own investment. Though perhaps counter-intuitive, it is true. Should you need an additional way of framing the conversations with these investors, ask them if they may very well be unintentionally pre-disposing your company (and their investment) to failure? In the end, any progress you make with existing investors to fix a toxic situation is better than no progress, no matter how tough the discussions.

One final comment on toxic rounds in general, in light of a financial downturn. A down-round or a flat-round is not necessarily something you should think of as a toxic round when it is offered to save your company, as it is likely the one and only offer you have on the table.. Yes, it will have an impact on dilution and future possible raises, but not raising the funds during a company crisis simply on the basis that the deal is not ideal, is not a reason to reject an offer as you will compromise survival today vs. an uncertain fear in the future.

Stacked Convertibles, SAFEs, etc.

Toxic rounds can also occur when a founder takes on too many convertible notes (or SAFEs) between equity rounds even if these aren't obvious at first.

This 'conversion stack' creates a problem for various reasons, but most importantly, it creates a massive pain for you when there is a final conversion event. Think about it this way... if you have five convertible notes outstanding, totaling say $5 million, and then you raise a new round of say $5 million to $10 million, conversion of those notes into the round will make it challenging for new investors to achieve any ownership target.

Another complication occurs when you have to raise more money but you have outstanding convertibles. No investor will want to invest in you when it's not clear how much of the company will be available for you, as a founder, after conversion but before their investment. It gets even harder when you try and get your outstanding note holders to convert when there is no qualifying round to trigger conversion, so it'll end up having to be something you negotiate => read: not easy.

My colleague in SC's Legal Team, Guisela Figueredo adds: *When a company has stacked convertibles it's particularly important for the founders to monitor their expected dilution against the percentage of ownership that may be "safely" given away at the respective stages of the company's growth. This is easier with post-money cap convertibles because you can calculate the ownership allocation based on the cap price (assuming that the conversion event is an up round). For example, if you have 100% of the company's shares and you know that at this stage you can dilute up to 25% but you have already issued one SAFE round for $500k at $8M cap (6.25%) and another SAFE round for $1.5M at $10M cap (15%), then you actually only have 78.75% of the ownership left as you've already granted 21.25% via the SAFE's (6.25%+15%). Hence, if you really need to raise an additional convertible round before the equity event, you will need to ensure that the dilution stays at 3.75% max to avoid getting yourself in trouble.*

Lastly, the more convertibles you take, each with their unique provisions and requirements (such as different long-stop dates / time-stamps at which they convert), the harder it becomes to make decisions as a unified shareholder base. Depending on the terms of those convertibles, you might need to consider more variables than a founder with just traditional ordinary shares in their shareholder base.

The moral of the story isn't to not use convertible notes, but to avoid having more than two outstanding at any time.

Tranched Investments

A final form of toxic round is tranched investments — when an investment is split into one or more parts. In order for the company to receive the later parts of a tranched investment, it usually has to achieve goals or objectives set as part of the conditions of investment. A typical example of a tranche: the investor gives you half the investment amount up-front, and half the investment when your revenues reach X amount.

Generally speaking, the current thinking about tranches by most investors is that they are a good tool to motivate founders to reach a milestone or, to reduce their exposure to risk. However, tranches are more damaging to the long-term success of a company than investors may think, particularly if milestones are not met or the company comes dangerously close to meeting them.

Specifically, I think tranches can:

- De-motivate founders and potentially reduce a founder's drive (according to Daniel H. Pink's view[17] of extrinsic motivation[18] — see below for more on this).
- Reduce a founding team's creativity regarding how to grow the business in a way that might be better for the long-term, but which in the short-term fails to achieve the next pre-determined milestone. (Think of a company sticking with a product in the hopes of hitting a deadline rather than pivoting, ultimately sticking with a product that will not yield maximum returns in the long run.)

---

[17] http://www.danpink.com/

[18] https://en.wikipedia.org/wiki/Motivatio

- Reduce good behavior (read: cheating to hit numbers). If someone really needs the cash, the temptation to cut corners can be strong.
- Promote "sandbagging" by the investor rather than full commitment.
- Create a self-fulfilling prophecy. In the words of the former CEO of Zemanta, Bostjan Spetic: "The cash you are raising is usually what you need to get to a significant milestone, like breakeven. Tying that budget to sub-milestones implicitly reduces the chances of actually hitting the big milestone, because it increases the risk of running out of cash prematurely."
- Create an accelerated cash burn to achieve the goal, which leaves the company in a vulnerable position for subsequent fundraising.
- Make the company toxic for an interested investor if the company doesn't receive the tranche from its existing investors.

As a founder, what do you say to an investor who's hell-bent on implementing tranches in your term sheet?

The best solution is to get a dialogue going to agree on one of the following three alternatives:

1. **Reduce the amount of money and target a closer-term milestone for the startup to achieve**. Yes, this implies that if the startup hits its milestone, it may command a higher valuation and the investor will not have been able to secure the economics of a tranched investment. But in exchange, the investor is getting a higher probability of overall success for their investment. Note: this should

not constitute an opportunity for predatory investors to underfund a company by picking a too-early milestone for founders to accomplish. This not only hurts the company's likelihood of achieving it, but also its likelihood of being able to secure follow-on capital.

2. **If an investor really needs to have tranches, implement "binary" milestones that are simple and clear**. What you want to avoid are tranches that have partial or subjective achievement, such as when a company comes pretty close to hitting its revenue figure or number of users. An example of an ideal binary milestone would be: you get a sum of money unlocked equaling the salary of a new CFO when you hire that CFO. The target is clear (hire CFO); you either hire the CFO or you don't.

3. **If you can't agree on either of the above, that implies either the company is overvalued or the investor may be overly cautious.** If the latter is true, the founder might want to reconsider taking them on as an investor (assuming he or she has a choice).

One more thought on why the carrot/stick theory behind tranches doesn't work. In his book *Drive*[19], author Daniel H. Pink walks through classical motivation models and compares them to his observations on actual motivation. He makes a very compelling case for companies, managers, parents, and just about everyone to rethink their preconceived notions on motivation, particularly around old carrot/stick methods.

Pink argues that carrot/stick, old-school motivation techniques fail for one of three reasons:

---

[19] https://www.danpink.com/books/drive/

1. **They don't mesh with the way many new business models are organizing what we do.** We are intrinsically motivated to maximize purpose, not profit.
2. **They don't comport with the way 21st-century economics thinks about what we do**. Economists are finally realizing that we're full-fledged human beings, not single-minded economic robots.
3. **It's hard to reconcile them with much of what we actually do at work.** For a growing number of people, work is often creative, interesting, and self-directed rather than unrelentingly routine, boring, and other-directed.

This topic may yield contrasting views on the efficacy of tranches by investors, but I sit squarely on the side that believes tranches, as they are generally used, are more value dilutive than value accretive for all parties involved.

13

Managing the Legal Process

The Importance of Good Legal Counsel

Entering into any new legal agreement is scary, but legal documents are part of business life. Your business's "brush with the law" doesn't have to cause paranoia though, particularly when you've been able to bring a good legal firm on board. Good legal counsel can help you understand all the tools in the legal toolbox: what they are for, how they are used, when they are appropriate and what they are protecting you against.

Now, when I say "good legal counsel", I don't mean your cousin's best friend who is a lawyer and can do it on the cheap. Cutting corners on legal counsel is probably the single worst thing you can do and will prevent you from starting off on the right foot with your investors since you'll end up wasting their time and yours. One sure sign of a startup ecosystem being mature is the availability of top-tier legal firms in the area. If you need to move the legal state of your company to get access to these, do so. You won't regret it. If you don't know where to start, cold-call a startup you admire and ask around.

In summary, good legal counsel does the following:

- **Validates your company.** The best firms are selective about their clientele. Their time is valuable, as is their reputation. Working with a top tier firm definitively says something about your company.
- **Saves money**. Yes, it sounds counter-intuitive, but while you may pay more in fees, reducing issues encountered during negotiation and avoiding problems that arise due to bad legal advice will mean you pay less in the long run.
- **Saves time.** An experienced lawyer is much more effective at drafting and reviewing documentation that a lawyer who

is getting acquainted with the docs on your time and dime. Additionally, that time could be better spent helping you think of what realistic scenarios you are trying to protect yourself against rather than making mountains out of molehills about standard terms.
- **Helps you consider the future.** Your company will go through many permutations throughout its life and a good, experienced lawyer will not only be able to help you with your current situation, but also prepare you for situations to come.
- **Good counsel knows the industry players.** By the very nature of being a top-tier legal firm, your lawyer(s) will know and have worked with top-tier investors firsthand. The firm will know what the investors tend to offer in their deals, what to expect as standard in their terms, and what might be out of the norm.

After considering the above, however, you do have to manage your counsel. In the end, you are responsible for every item on your documents. So, as much as great legal counsel can help you avoid making mistakes, don't slack off during the process. Stay engaged, pay attention to the details, and you'll learn a lot.

Managing the Flow of Documents

One of the most time-consuming things founders have to do other than raise money is deal with all the legal paperwork — pre- and post-investment offer— that fundraising typically generates. This phase can also be emotionally difficult, depending on how many items are being discussed before finalizing.

While there is no standard process (largely due to the variability in deal types and jurisdictional issues) that can be outlined for how to deal with your unique legal situation, I've proposed a few tips that will help you navigate this process.

1. Always be mindful that the most important thing you have at your disposal is your word. If you make promises, keep them. Create trust between yourself and everyone you deal with. Say what you mean and mean what you say, and ask questions if you're not sure. This will help build you a good reputation.
2. If you aren't incorporated yet, or if you've just started working on an idea with friends, agree on pre-founder and advisor arrangements (relating to equity splits and vesting) before lawyers start drafting stuff . Lawyers often need to change docs several times to accommodate founders changing their minds or negotiations taking a different turn. We've shared a document on Seedsummit.org called The Founder's Collaboration Agreement, which you can use if you don't have something like this.
3. Always check what your legal responsibilities with existing shareholders are before making any decisions with or without them. Make sure to keep them involved and inform them of any information about the new round if it is regarding whatever rights they may have as part of their investment documentation. If this means you need to ask them something, ask them—but don't leave it to the last minute.
4. Generally speaking, conversations are founder-to-investor and lawyer-to-lawyer, meaning you rarely speak to the investor's counsel directly and vice versa. Tom

McGinn adds: "*All-party meetings, where everyone is involved, are generally a huge waste of time. If their client is on the call, many lawyers end up posturing and fighting points their client shouldn't really care about. Generally, the most efficient way to run the process is (i) to have a clear commercial agreement between the principals, (ii) let the lawyers draft the documents to reflect that agreement, and (iii) for any commercial point that arises during the drafting to be discussed between the principals.*"

5. Don't be annoying: lawyers cost money for both sides of the table.

    a) Do your own research and aggregate your questions as much as possible so that retained counsel for all parties is used efficiently.

    b) Make sure you have a position on all items that are being discussed so you don't go back and forth on stuff over the phone or after decisions have been made. Nothing is more annoying than backtracking during legal processes.

6. Manage your legal team: Don't let your lawyer get annoying or overly aggressive with your investor. The investor can always walk away if you and your counsel come across as difficult or ask for stuff that might actually be destructive for the company in their view. Be assertive, for sure, but don't be divisive.

    a) Seek to understand the issues and think creatively about how to solve problems, rather than letting your lawyers get into a stalemate or argument with your potential investor. Always feel free to say "Let's park this point for now and return to it after we've had time to consider it."

    b) Don't let paranoia about what others could do to

screw you get the better of you. It is okay to be slightly paranoid, but don't let it get so bad that you make the legal process feel painful as you come up with bogus reasons to reject perfectly common clauses in an investor's proposed documentation.

Tom McGinn, shares: "*I think this last point is key. Particularly in early-stage investments, the documents should, while faithful to the business principle in the term sheet, generally be as close to the NVCA/BVCA form documents (or a simplified version thereof) as possible. Speed, faithful implementation of the business deal and a set of documents that round's investors are familiar with (and can be rolled forward as part of the next funding round) should be the goal. I've seen many examples of founders (and less sophisticated investors) getting freaked out by a horror scenario that is incredibly unlikely to occur that ends up driving up costs and reducing social capital with the investors and other shareholders.*"

7. As we covered in the term sheet section, legal documents have various parts, both commercial (valuations, percentages, etc.) and legal (jurisdiction, filing/reporting procedures, etc.). Get as many commercial points as possible agreed between you and the investor before involving the lawyers (This is effectively what the term sheet is, but sometimes some stuff slips into the subsequent docs to keep the term sheet "light".) Leave lawyers to just represent these on your documents. If you need to have a discussion on a commercial point, do it with your investor alone and offline (even if you have to ask your lawyer or another shareholder for advice separately). You shouldn't spend time on the phone with lawyers negotiating commercial points as lawyers will help you

through the technical points.

Tom McGinn adds: *"This is particularly relevant if you're a first-time founder. It's worth getting sophisticated early-stage counsel involved at the term sheet stage so they can (i) help you think through the commercial deal (e.g. who should have negative control over key decisions and who should have negative control over operational decisions), (ii) make sure there's nothing in the term sheet that cuts across that, and (iii) advise you on what they're seeing in the market (e.g. is it a normal request that voluntary resignation is a Bad Leaver limb, should all optionees have double trigger acceleration, etc.?)"*

8. Always "red line" any changes you make to documents and keep track of all changes. Use Track Changes on Word/Docs, etc. Remember, you can always use the "Compare" feature on Word/Docs to identify any changes from one document to the next if it has not been red-lined.

9. Always seek solutions. There are multiple ways to skin a cat. Any issue can usually be solved with a thoughtful and creative approach. The lawyers aren't there to come up with solutions for you—they're just there to articulate your creative solutions in legal terms.

10. DO propose using standard documentation that other lawyers have frequently seen. In the US consider using the Series Seed docs or YC's SAFE, or the Seedsummit docs in Europe. Familiarize yourself with a few versions of standardized documents, and ask if the ones your lawyer is using are based on these standards—which will reduce everyone's workload.

11. Manage the closing process. When there are multiple angels involved, lawyers often spend a lot of time getting

signatures which increases costs that founders don't want to pay. Sometimes, you, as the founder, can handle this, but the best case is if one of the leading angels takes charge of this process. If you don't have a highly organized person on board, be prepared to take the lead. Tom McGinn adds: *"In the UK, there are very few documents that should be executed as a deed anymore and good counsel will generally try to avoid deeds as much as possible (also because it makes it harder to sign the document electronically). Totally agreed re the founders being able to save costs (and look good in front of their investors) if they pick up parts of the deal themselves, particularly parts that don't require legal advice (e.g. the disclosure process—which is essentially an entirely factual exercise—and the closing process)."*

12. Do your due diligence. Get your IP agreements, employment agreements, etc. organized to help the process go faster and smoother for your new investor, as they will likely have to review these documents.
13. Keep calm at all times. If you lose it, you risk losing the investor.

The Closing & Funds Transfer

Once you have completed the key legal documents and any necessary due diligence the investor may require, the money comes in and the hard work starts.

Make sure you send investors the necessary international banking codes and also send them the ZIP/PDF version of all signed documents. Don't make people chase you!

Bonus 1: SeedLegals

If you are in the EU area, you might have heard of SeedLegals, a company started by my friend Anthony Rose. If your company is in its early stages, it might be a worthwhile platform to use for your early rounds. It will save you some of the hassle of the points I brought up in this chapter, as well as some of the admin of managing many investors (particularly if you have many angels).

More on SeedLegals in their words:

> SeedLegals was founded by serial entrepreneur Anthony Rose and serial angel investor Laurent Laffy, who met at a party in Rome. They'd both had enough of paying insane amounts of money to lawyers for the same legal documents at every funding round, and funding rounds taking months to negotiate and close. They decided to change it.
>
> Fast forward six months and SeedLegals launched as the world's first platform that lets founders and investors easily create, negotiate and sign all the legal agreements they need to do a funding round. In less than three years, SeedLegals is now the largest closer of funding rounds in the UK.

Bonus 2: Where Should I Incorporate?

The reason why this question comes up is often because there are different benefits of being incorporated in different locations. Founders can find themselves pulled in different directions, especially since they can receive conflicted advice from well-intentioned advisors. Some of the issues founders may be balancing as they decide where to incorporate include things like tax breaks or penalties, local grants, and paperwork. This is particularly the case when they are thinking that the US might be where they will end up in the future.

Below are some issues you should consider when making a decision about incorporation. I am not recommending a specific jurisdiction for incorporation.

Let's start by stating that, for the most part, incorporation decisions aren't necessarily permanent. Tom McGinn adds: "*Generally, the sooner you flip jurisdictions, the simpler this will be (as the simpler the company's corporate, operational and capitalization structure will be). You can also "effectively flip" by having your subsidiary become the key operational company. There are a number of high-profile examples of UK companies in the US doing this, and vice versa. If you think there's a possibility you may flip, it's worth including language in your documents to allow the board and some majority of shareholders to have the right to do this on behalf of all shareholders (so long as all shareholders are treated equally by the flip) (to avoid smaller shareholders having a veto over what is a key strategic decision.*"

Following from Tom's point, certain circumstances can make it difficult for you to flip your company (take your company from one legal jurisdiction to another), but for the most part, you can almost always find a way to move your company later if it benefits you to do so. Generally, the cost of doing this will be proportional to its complexity and the legal jujitsu your lawyers will need in order to make this happen. So while incorporation in a particular place doesn't have to be permanent, changing it can be a headache, and you should carefully consider your options before taking the easiest or most obvious route.

Now that you perhaps feel a bit more "relieved" about the not-so-permanent nature of your decision, let's look at some key factors to consider:

1. **Tax implications and tax treaties.** One major factor in your and your investors' returns, now and in the future, is whether there will be a tax impact to you, your employees and co-founders. Consider the following : is their tax relief on returns as a founder? What happens if you flip to a different geography in the future? What are the income tax as well as capital gains liabilities (NB: links are to a UK site, but the definitions are not geographically specific) Does the jurisdiction have negative tax implications for your future investors? These questions can sometimes be answered by tax specialists from within your lawyer's firm, or your accountants.
2. **Investor implications**. As mentioned above, another reason why the jurisdiction matters is because investors will optimize based on what the tax implications are for them and may prefer jurisdictions where investing in your company provides tax relief. Additionally, there are matters in the final legal docs which they may prefer dealing with in their local jurisdiction rather than in new, less familiar ones.
3. **Paperwork**. Paperwork is clearly one of the biggest headaches of making this decision. This includes the interval in which you need to report, as well as other requirements, such as company filings and approvals. For example, Germany has some unique 'friction' attributes on this matter that other countries do not have.
4. **Residency**. Some geographies may have a residency

requirement for founders. Keep this in mind, particularly if you don't have the appropriate immigration status or obtaining it is difficult.

5. **Human resources**. It may be harder for your employees to move, if necessary, in certain countries, and/or hiring might also be problematic due to lack of human capital. Additionally, there may be restrictions on how you can hire/fire employees that might affect how you upscale/-downscale your employees. João Abiul Menano of James suggests: "One should also consider tax on labor. In some cases, a tax incentive given to an early-stage startup can help to keep the burn rate low (more important even for companies in which labor costs account for between 70 percent and 90 percent of monthly expenses)."

6. **Governance**. Corporate Governance requirements tend to vary from country to country and thus may also be affected by where you are incorporated. Certain company governance structures are enforced on your company depending on where you incorporate and investors may have an opinion on that one way or another. Since you'll have to abide by these requirements, you might as well familiarize yourself with these variables before making your decision. Tom McGinn adds: "*I think this is a key point—US law (and to a lesser extent UK law) are less rigid than most continental European jurisdictions, meaning that the company can be set up and run in a way that is more in line with whatever the commercial deal is between the company and key investors (e.g. in terms of who has negative control, which shareholders get information rights and pre-emption rights, etc.). For example, in many European jurisdictions, it will be difficult/impossible to set up your documents in a way*

that includes the flip mechanism described above."

7. **M&A**. Your company will eventually get sold or merged or floated. In some countries, this process is straightforward, simple, and easy for potential acquirers to understand and do quickly. In other countries, the process may be less well-known and may cause delays or complications.
8. **Free information availability**. Although you will likely have a lawyer helping you through many of these topics, it's always great when you can learn on your own from others' experiences. Some jurisdictions have more founders sharing on forums and the like, relaying how they overcame their specific problems. This can be a very valuable way of reducing your cost to learn and thus reducing your legal costs.

Having reviewed all of these issues with your current and/or future shareholders, you should at least have a better starting point to make a well thought-out decision.

For more on this topic, visit Dan Glazer's blog post on this. It is THE *Bible* on this subject: https://medium.com/@daniel.glazer/u-s-expansion-and-fundraising-a-comprehensive-faq-3bf143cd5249

14

Conclusion

Hopefully you have found this book to be a good starting point to arm you with the right information to begin your fundraising journey. The road ahead will be filled with twists and turns, ups and downs. You might be one of the fortunate ones who raises quickly, or you might be scattered with many rejections before you finally get to a yes, but don't lose faith during this process.

There is a Japanese word, *kaizen*, that translates as "seeking constant improvement". No failure is truly a failure unless you learn nothing from it.

Best wishes and thank you for reading!
  Carlos Espinal

III

Appendix — Additions to the First Edition

15

Get Your Elephant in the Room Under Control!

As covered earlier in this book— presentations can sometimes have an "Elephant in the Room." When presenting/pitching, do you know and can you spot your company's "Elephant in the room"? From our favorite online encyclopedia:

> *The expression "the elephant in the room" is a metaphorical idiom in English for an important or enormous topic, question, or controversial issue that is obvious or that everyone knows about but no one mentions or wants to discuss because it makes at least some of them uncomfortable and is personally, socially, or politically embarrassing, controversial, inflammatory, or dangerous. The metaphorical elephant represents an obvious problem or difficult situation that people do not want to talk about.*

It is based on the idea/thought that something as conspicuous as an elephant can appear to be overlooked in codified social interactions and that the sociology/psychology of repression also operates on the macro scale. Various languages around the world have words that describe similar concepts.

I love this expression because it's so obvious. How could you NOT notice something so big within a confined space? And yet, sometimes we do ignore it, or at least fail to acknowledge it. When it comes to pitching your company, it's not unusual for you to have an "Elephant in the Room" and, funnily enough, it's often easier to ignore it (out of fear), rather than confront it head on.

Why is this important?

Usually, your Elephant is something that's perhaps awkward to be up front about For example, a like-for-like competitor already in the market, or that several companies like yours have failed in the past, or there is a big player out there who owns most of the market.

I've received many presentations over the years and have observed how others hear and perceive them. What inevitably happens is when you ignore that Elephant, it grows in your audience's mind. It grows to the point where it consumes their entire mind space. The points you are trying to make get lost because the audience is actively trying to suppress their desire to confront the Elephant with "How about X?" which has been festering in their minds the entire time!

Whether you address it directly or indirectly, you need to address it sooner rather than later. The solution is simple: you have to realize that this Elephant isn't real. It's merely a blow-up elephant and one you can easily deflate if addressed early on in your presentation. People will either agree with the way you deflated it or not, but you'll at least be able to move past it.

How do you identify your Elephant?

Unless you are willing to delude yourself, you likely already know what it is. It may be a question investors or friends have repeatedly asked you when you explain what you are working on. It usually starts with something like "Isn't that like...?" or "Didn't that...?" or something like that. In short, if you are feeling uncomfortable about something, most likely that's your Elephant.

How do you deflate your Elephant?

Through logic. The fact is, you would not have started working on your business if you didn't have good reason to believe this Elephant was not going to hurt you in the long run. If it's a competitor everyone asks you about, you can simply talk about how you are tackling things differently and serving a different need/customer. If it's a sector that has had many deaths in the past, perhaps talk about how the timing is different now versus then, and really delve deep into why that is the case. For example, one of our companies, Thriva, helps you take control of your health and find out what's happening inside your body with a simple finger-prick blood test. When the founders went out to pitch, it was around the time Theranos was imploding, and there were enough "perceived" similarities that pitching without addressing that case as specifically different (and how) simply led to an eventual outburst later by someone with the obvious question. Naturally, the founder was on to this, and addressed all the key points of differentiation early on.

In conclusion, to move past an Elephant, you simply need to present sound logic as to why the Elephant doesn't apply to you; any reason is better than no reason at all!

16

Weatherproofing Your Startup for any Financial Climate

This chapter helps you with a perspective on what can happen during tough times and what you might be able to do about it, particularly if you find yourself fundraising during these times in the future (as I hope this book serves founders for many years to come!).

Bad things happen. During my career, I've had the chance to witness four economically challenging times (the 2001, 2008, 2020, and 2022/2023 bumps). In the first, I was in a startup (Baltimore Technologies) and in the second, I was in a VC fund (Doughty Hanson) and now, I'm at Seedcamp. I can still remember the serial layoffs when I was at Baltimore Technologies as things started to come to a head. One after the other, in the order of the desks we had, we went to receive our separation packages. It was a sad day for many of us and it taught me quite a bit about how quickly things can go south. (I still remember chats I had with my colleagues only a few months prior regarding the value of our options as the CEO had promised much more growth and aggressive expansion).

During my time at Doughty Hanson, I experienced a downturn from a different point of view. Many of our companies — along with those of many other VCs — were going through the same challenges and I noticed a pattern started to emerge. While not exhaustive, I noticed the following six attributes:

1. Public companies stop acquiring external companies and start focusing on reducing costs internally.
2. Because of #1 above, exit opportunities for companies (M&A and IPOs) that rely on external funding for growth or returns start drying up.
3. As VCs start to focus their funds on rescue "bridge" rounds for existing portfolio companies that are of high value, less money (to zero money) is directed to new investments.
4. Massive failures in growth-sized startups start generating other massive failures as accounts payable aren't paid and accounts receivable are received. The whole "chain", so to speak, starts unraveling.
5. With some failures being quite nasty, regulators come under pressure to take action, which then drives audits and governance clampdowns in startups.
6. Funds start struggling as their portfolios haven't received enough funding to survive #3 above, so new investments start to dry up.

If the above sounds scary, it's because it **is** scary. However, many of the best companies were born or chiseled out of tough times because of the actions and mindsets their founders brought to the circumstance, and because some of the market dynamics also changed in their favor due to the downturn's impact. Mark Roberge —the Chief Revenue Officer of HubSpot, a Boston-based inbound marketing firm, and Senior Lecturer at Harvard Business School as well as at Stage 2 Capital —wrote a great piece on the opportunities that can surface in a downturn and that he experienced during his time. Read it here—A Recession Doesn't Mean Your Startup Can't Grow

So, a downturn can be good for you as well as bad for you, but what can you do today? In the words of friend and Venture Partner Emeritus at Seedcamp Stephen Allott, *"If you have the capital you can double down and beat the other players, and if you're not lean and mean, you'll either die, or get forced into being lean and mean."*

In that spirit, while not an exhaustive list, below are some actions that you could consider should we all find ourselves in that situation in the future. In a bull market, some of these actions will seem contrary to what is being popularly proposed for massive and fast growth (usually expensive paid growth)! However, these actions should not be seen as being more "conservative or risk averse". Rather, they are about being more robust in your growth strategy, regardless of the market conditions!

These actions include:

1. **While the going is good, go for cash-generative customers over vanity customers** — there are customers and then there are customers. Those who pay on time and have good solid financing are always going to trump those who represent pie-in-the-sky opportunities or who will flake

on contracts due to their own situations failing.

2. **Lock in contracts and get pre-payments via discounts if you can** — by focusing on getting cash-in-hand, even if at the cost of some discounts, you make sure you aren't putting yourself in a position where a customer can flake on you later in the year if things get worse.

3. **Make sure you're not overspending internally** — hey, we are all suckers for great startup merch and furniture, but do you really need to spend that much on office perks and other cash-draining activities? Keeping things lean means you have fewer cash commitments, and you also won't have the issue of having employee morale drop massively as previously indulgent Massage Mondays perks get removed.

4. **Focus on becoming cash-flow positive** — at the end of the day, nothing beats being cash-flow positive, particularly if your customers are counter-cyclical or somewhat immune to the cycle (e.g. government services, larger cash-rich companies, etc.). Short of that, focus on sustainable growth, not growth through crazy spend on customer acquisition.

5. **Make focusing on receivables management a top management focus** — *"Lead from the top with questions like Have we been paid? What do we have to do to get paid? Have we done it yet? Who is accountable end to end for getting this customer to pay?"* — Stephen Allott

6. **Raise as much cash as you can (within reason)** — nothing beats having cash on hand, so the more you can raise, the more "reserved" you will be for tough times ahead. Or course, we've already covered what happens when it is too much, so this is more about balanced cash reserves

and one where you're planning for the appropriate use of this cash, not just a spend-quick mentality.
7. **Take money from the right investors** - When times are good, many investors compete against one another simply by 'how much' cash they can give you. Beyond a certain point where you've meet your cash needs, focus on the 'right' investor vs. the one who offers the most cash and/or best valuation, for during a downturn, you will need support and guidance.

Ivan Farneti, an ex-colleague of mine at Doughty Hanson and now Founding Partner at Five Seasons Ventures (a food-tech-focused venture fund), who had to navigate some of the portfolio issues of both previous downturns, had this to add: *"Because of the length of this run, most of the founders in VCs' portfolios have not seen a downturn before. They may not be prepared, and knee-jerk reactions like cutting the online marketing budget and letting go of their community manager may be amongst some of the moves they make, but they may not be the right moves long term. Experienced board members should step in and add real value here (not just financial controls, but also how to deliver those cuts, but rather what communication style to use, how to manage it, etc.). Additionally, founders may want to know where they stand in the priority stack of the portfolio of their investors, and may want to know how much reserves are left with their name written on them. Naturally, VCs might not want to share this with all of them, but this information could be important to help decide on alternatives when there may be still time."*

As mentioned before, some of the above recommendations might sound heretical to advice given to startups during a bull market where there is a fast spend/grow attitude and cash-rich environment, but keep in mind that almost a decade ago, Bill Gurley wrote a great piece to his companies on how to weather that storm and Sequoia sent out a deck[20] to its companies — and many of the same points that were made then are still valid today; there is a reason why great advice stands the test of time! To add to that, Accel recently shared an article called Control Your Growth, Control Your Future that's equally worth reading.

---

[20] https://www.sequoiacap.com/wp-content/uploads/sites/6/2022/06/Adapting-to-Endure_Sequoia-Capital-2022.pdf

17

Deciphering Crowdfunding

Back in August 2020, Andy Shovel and Pete Sharman, co-founders of Seedcamp company THIS, launched an equity crowdfunding campaign. The alternative meat startup aimed to raise £2 million on top of the £5.6 million they had previously received from Seedcamp and a handful of other funds. One month after launching the campaign, THIS had doubled its funding goal. They brought on board 1,844 investors to raise a total of £4.5 million (and in a record time of just 15 hours!).

THIS's story is becoming less and less unusual. One of the funding sources that founders like Andy and Pete are increasingly able to tap above and beyond VC and angel funding is crowdfunding via online platforms such as Kickstarter , AngelList, and Seedrs, to name a few. However, these platforms are not all the same.

To help better categorize the use cases for the different types of crowdfunding platforms, let's split them into two:

1. Cash for Product Pre-Orders: Kickstarter, Indiegogo, etc.
2. Cash for Equity: AngelList (US and UK), Seedrs (UK),

Crowdcube (UK), and newcomers like Odin, etc.

We won't delve too deeply into the first category, but in summary, these platforms are used primarily to help fund the pre-order of tech product inventory, while other sources of cash will still be needed to fund the operational aspects of your company. This doesn't mean, of course, that this is the only way people use cash raised on these types of platforms, but this is how it is generally used.

To highlight the above concept, let's take a look at the stats on Kickstarter's site (data from Jan 2024; for updated data visit https://www.kickstarter.com/help/stats). With some number-crunching, what you can see is an interesting set of conclusions.

1. The bulk of successful projects are raising around $1,000 to $20,000 on Kickstarter, with only a relative minority (4.5% percent) of successfully completed projects raising in excess of $100,000. (FYI, this is a 2x rise from 2014 at the time of the first edition of this book.
2. Technology projects as a whole, no matter what the size, only represent 4.87 percent of the successfully completed projects on Kickstarter. The highest success rates are Games, Music, Film and Video, and Art in that order. As a matter of fact, out of 15 categories, Tech is 8th on the list, with Journalism being the least-backed project type, just below Dance.
3. The highest success brackets for technology projects is between $20,000 and $99,999 raised, with the brackets above and below this range having half as many successful projects.
4. In the unsuccessfully funded projects category, Technol-

ogy is third of the total projects after Film & Video and Games, with a whopping 11.34 percent of tech projects being unfunded, almost equal to that of Publishing projects, which come in fourth place.
5. Raising over $1 million on Kickstarter for Technology projects is just not really going to play in your favor, with an overall success rate of less than 1 percent (this was the case both in 2014 and 2021).

That said, the largest outlier and most well-known tech Kickstarter fundraise was that of one of my favorite products at the time, the Pebble Smartwatch , with over $10 million pledged. The Pebble team still raised capital from VCs and angels. Meanwhile, likely one of the most famous being Oculus which raised $2.5M on Kickstarter and two years later were acquired by Facebook for over $2B! I'll let you draw your own conclusions from these outliers.

For the second category of crowdfunding platforms you start seeing a different trend, one of fundraising designed to help you build and scale your company rather than just to help you build a product.On these platforms, rather than having your contributors provide cash in exchange for a promise or a pre-purchase of a product, the contributors are getting a "share" of your company. Literally, they are becoming investors and shareholders, with all the pros and cons that entails. What differentiates all major platforms in this category is how they structure the investment into your company and where they can operate.

In the UK, one of the most successful companies with this model is Seedrs. To provide you some perspective on them:

In 2023, their average round size for all campaigns on the platform was £1.3m while the median raise for seed stage businesses (those with a pre-money valuation of less than £1m) was £197k. Of all the campaigns on Seedrs last year, 88 percent had a success rate of completion. However, of all the applicants to Seedrs per year, approximately only 1 percent are accepted onto the platform. In total, 266 businesses were funded in 2023.

There are ways to maximize your chances of success raising money on platforms like Seedrs. Having spoken with their team, they shared their advice on what it takes to successfully raise.

Firstly they advise that if you don't have an engaged community of users or are not in a compelling sector that's of interest to many investors, you will struggle to hit your funding target regardless.

Secondly, to get rounds going, you will need an anchor investor. This anchor could be a single lead investor or a group of individuals in your network, and will aim to fund 30-40 percent of your round target size if you want to increase the likelihood of success (although there is no magic starting percentage). Seedrs, through their networks, shine best in leveraging that "start" and driving the remaining amount, with their connections to capital providers and what comes through their co-marketing they raise with you.

While valuations are always a subject of much debate as time goes on, Seedrs lets the founders and lead investors determine round dynamics. They will only step in with information to help the company if valuations are outside market norms and will lead to a bad outcome when exposed to their community.

What's interesting is that, unlike with Kickstarter, Tech is something that does well on Seedrs, with 46 successful campaigns last year. One of the main non-tech sectors that is super popular is food and beverage. One example is Allplants, the startup building the home of plant-based food. They have raised three times on Seedrs including in 2021 when they raised £22m from 834 investors and in 2023 when they raised £5.4m from 572 investors. Tech companies addressing key problems in society, such as environmental issues or consumer fintech (Monzo/Revolut) tend to also do well. In particular, ClimateTech is a big sector of interest for Seedrs investors. The Seedrs 2022 Sector Report which analysed more than 324 campaigns, found that ClimateTech thrived with investment growing 154% from £15.7m to £40.1m that year, with 58% more businesses raising from 37% more investors.

Once accepted on the Seedrs platform, it can take about 3-4 months to get your business funded. The first 1-1.5 months is spent getting investment-ready to go public on the platform. This is followed by a month of being "live" and open for investment on the platform and then another 1-1.5 months to close out the round. Naturally, the fewer investors you have investing outside Seedrs, the faster it can go, and the more you have, the longer it can drag out, as all participating investors have to fill out key documents and naturally transfer funds (those investing through Seedrs are all looked after by the platform).

In terms of how rounds are structured, Seedrs asks for standard pre-emption, drag-along and tag-along provisions, minority protections, and, lastly, information rights. None of these are surprising; after all, it's an equity investment into your company. Luckily, the platform aggregates investors, so that you only deal with them as a composite/group/whole and not 100+ in the same way.

Some final things they suggest to consider as part of a campaign on Seedrs include:

- Crowdfunding is something to consider in conjunction with a syndicated round or a VC/institution leading the round.
- Having a community is super necessary for the success of your raise as they will help amplify your message and get you the support you need. If you don't have one yet, start working on it before you crowd fund.
- Crowdfunding is not easy money. Expect to have to put in a lot of work in setting it up and managing it.
- The largest benefit of crowdfunding is the marketing element it supports you with, and the long-term customer engagement and loyalty created by investors becoming customers.
- Crowdfunding is NOT a place to go if you want to go down the path of silly high valuations.
- Crowdfunding platforms in your local geography can usually benefit from structures that offer tax relief for their investors, driving demand for your company. (Seedrs in the UK benefits from SEIS and EIS structures for angel investors.)

Final things to consider

When considering a crowdfunding platform, make sure your research explores the following:

- How does the investment size fit with your cash and growth needs?
- How much would you like to raise on a platform vs. outsides investors who are not on the platform (and how to intermingle the two within a reasonable timeframe to a close)?
- What are the fees associated with going through the platform?
- Will you be able to secure the right supplementary investors to make sure your project is successful?
- What have been the success rates for your type of company (industry) and product?
- How does the platform structure the investment coming into your company (lest you find yourself with a cap table laden with investors and a tricky governance structure)?
- Is crowdfunding suitable for your raise, and/or will you get out of it what you think you will?

Crowdfunding as a way of either funding your product or your company's growth is increasingly a trend that will supplement, and in some cases entirely replace, early-stage investment capital from institutional sources such as VCs. At the very least, you should consider building profiles on the relevant platforms for your location and industry.

18

Additional Resources

Cap Table Series with Felix Martinez & Carlos
Episode 1 - https://youtu.be/VdvjBs3VEHM
Episode 2 - https://youtu.be/mVFxtaXzG2o
Episode 3 - https://youtu.be/wEW2ubin9b4?si=8wscWqDJIHmE0TYn
(Check for further Episodes from within Youtube as they had not been published as of the writing of this book)

Legal Hour Series with Tom Wilson & Carlos
https://cee.medium.com/the-legal-hour-series-all-episodes-dbb79e4bbd36

How to get a meeting with investors by Robin Klein
https://medium.com/localglobe-notes/getting-your-foot-in-a-vc-s-door-19e1af30df6f

On raising too much capital:
https://sifted.eu/articles/raising-too-much-venture-capital

/

YC's Kirsty Nathoo on Safe's and Priced Equity Rounds:
https://www.youtube.com/watch?v=Dk6JNTDec9I

On building a financial model & why:
https://visible.vc/blog/financial-modeling-for-startups/

https://foundercollective.medium.com/why-do-vcs-really-want-to-see-your-financial-model-66b4e17cf07c

On building pitch decks:
https://techcrunch.com/2015/06/08/lessons-from-a-study-of-perfect-pitch-decks-vcs-spend-an-average-of-3-minutes-44-seconds-on-them/

https://business.tutsplus.com/articles/startup-pitch-deck-examples---cms-33037

On stock options and rewarding talent, from Index Ventures:
https://www.indexventures.com/resources/rewarding-talent/

And Balderton's Guide to Employee Equity:
https://www.balderton.com/wp-content/uploads/2021/02/Equity-Guide-Balderton-Capital-January-2020.pdf

A template pipeline for managing your fundraise:
http://bit.ly/2RKF4Ad

Legal Templates:

(US) https://www.seriesseed.com/
(EU) http://seedsummit.org/
(UK) https://www.bvca.co.uk/Policy/Tax-Legal-and-Regulatory/Industry-guidance-standardised-documents/Model-documents-for-early-stage-investments
(UK) https://seedlegals.com/resources/introducing-seedfast-an-seis-eis-friendly-way-to-raise-ahead-of-a-funding-round/
(US) https://www.ycombinator.com/documents/

On what Tier is your investor?
http://seedcamp.com/resources/what-tier-is-your-investor-or-what-to-look-for-in-an-investor/

A Practical Guide to Series A Fundraising: Part 1 & 2 by Kindred Capital
  https://blog.usejournal.com/a-practical-guide-to-series-a-fundraising-part-1-940f0616bb9b
  https://kindredcapital.medium.com/a-practical-guide-to-series-a-fundraising-part-2-969ea2e3e427

Control Your Growth / Control Your Future by Accel:
  https://www.accel.com/noteworthy/control-your-growth-control-your-future

Acknowledgments

Firstly, I'd like to thank all the founders I've had the chance to work with over the years. They have taught me so much through their courage and perseverance.

Colleagues

I'd also like to thank my friends and work/industry colleagues whose support has been instrumental in helping me draft this book's earliest revisions and its materials, either via a blog post, or just a simple idea or opinion. Thank you to Tina Baker, Reshma Sohoni, Philipp Moehring, Giles Hawkins, Dale Huxford, Sitar Teli, Ivan Farneti, Robin Klein, Alliott Cole, Ben Tompkins, Sean Seton-Rogers, Christoph Janz, Jason Ball, Vincent Jacobs, Christian Hernandez, Andy Chung, Eze Vidra, Sherry Coutu, Jeff Lynn, Scott Sage, and Nick Verkroost.

Book Support & Publishing Support

A special thanks to team Reedsy: Emmanuel Nataf, Ricardo Fayet, and Matt Cobb. This whole thing would not have been possible without you guys!

Additionally a big thanks to Miguel Pinho (who very kindly helped me with the book's v1 website) and Matt Cobb, more on him below (who helped me with this book's current website and cover art).

Cover Art

I would like to extend my heartfelt gratitude to Matt Cobb, the talented artist and co-founder of Reedsy, responsible for all the artwork featured in the book, including the three book covers (v1, v2, v3). It's worth noting that Matt drew inspiration primarily from our conversations.

In the initial version, we discussed the metaphor of fundraising resembling mountain climbing, with various 'camps' representing different stages. Interestingly, at the time of the first edition, there was no concept of a pre-seed stage. However, by the time the second edition came around, not only had the pre-seed stage emerged, but round sizes had also expanded significantly. This led to some anxiety about the growing size of seed stage rounds. Consequently, the cover art depicted an 'x' on the termsheet instead of an actual number, and the color scheme adopted a darker tone, possibly reflecting the impending challenges in the venture markets. Additionally, and on a humorous note, I think the character on the front cover, whilst representing a founder, were modelled after me (hence the balding and then the subsequent hat in the latest version). In the current and final edition, we returned to the original concept, placing less emphasis on monetary terms and refocusing on the idea of a series of camps along the fundraising journey.

I have truly appreciated the outstanding work that Matt has

contributed and his artistic vision for the book. Thank you, Matt!

Notable Manuscript Contributions

Thank you to Devin Hunt & Stephen Allott for helping me review the section on valuations and for your wisdom over the years. Thank you Tom McGinn for the support with the legal review.

A huge thank you to **David Ola** & **Kate McGinn** for the amazing support with the second revision. You took it from Alpha to Beta! Another huge thank you to **Millan Suri** & **Daniel Inge** for picking up the baton from David & Kate and helping me get restarted, and lastly and with much appreciate for their massive efforts, a big thank you to **Will Bennett** & **Amber Patel** for taking it from Beta to 'release' with this third version. Your collective wisdom, input, proof reading, and patience not only gave me perspective, but also a better feel for questions left unanswered. I will forever be appreciative of your efforts.

Editing Support

The Reedsy Platform allows you to find and work with editors and many other publishing professionals. I'd like to thank the editors of each version of this book for their contributions and insights to make the book read 'good' ;)

- Marie Timell – Version 3
- Helen Castell – Version 2
- Rebecca Faith Heyman – Version 1

Mentors

Lastly, but not "leastly", I'd like to also thank the mentors who were instrumental in my personal journey and who have helped in my understanding of much of the material contained herein. Thank you to Walter Urbaniak, Adam Lipson, George Powlick, Nigel Grierson, Michael J. Skok, Soren Hein, Stefan Tirtey, Jerry Ennis, Turi Munthe, Saul Klein, Chris Grew, Gabbi Cahane, and many others who have given me feedback and help over the years.

How This Book Was Made

In the Spring of 2014, I had the opportunity to meet Emmanuel Nataf, one of the founders of Reedsy.com, a marketplace for authors to meet publishing industry professionals. I was impressed by Emmanuel's ambition to disrupt a huge industry with a new way of thinking about how, via a marketplace, all these parties could meet and work together and change how books are written. We invested in Emmanuel and his co-founders Ricardo and Matt's company a few months later to help them achieve their vision.

In terms of my personal journey writing this book, shortly after investing in Reedsy, the idea of aggregating all my blog posts from http://www.thedrawingboard.me and creating a book became more "possible" as I further understood the world of self-publishing through my initial chats with the founders of Reedsy. Shortly after our first conversations, Emmanuel and Ricardo introduced me to Rebecca Faith Heyman, one of the early editors on the platform, and through chatting with her and her guidance on the project, I decided to take a leap and write this book.

Insofar as tools are concerned, for the first edition, I used Scrivener to help me with the original drafting and organization of the book. After, to start off the editorial process, I transferred from Scrivener to Microsoft Word. This made it easier for my editor and I to track changes and update versions.

However, since then, Reedsy has created an online editor, which is how I edited and rewrote this new entire edition—the 2021 and 2023 edition.

Lastly, but massively importantly, I'm forever grateful to Matt Cobb, Reedsy co-founder and Lead Designer, for designing the aesthetics of the book itself, including the cover. I'd also like to thank Will Bennett and Millan Suri for their work in assisting on the editing of this edition.

If any of you reading this are considering writing your own content, do give the Reedsy platform a shot. I am biased, but I know I wouldn't have embarked on this project if it hadn't been for its platform.

About the Author

Carlos is Managing Partner at Seedcamp, the leading European seed fund launched in 2007 with a belief that European entrepreneurs have the power to compete on a global scale.

With investments in over 450 companies including many of the well-known European unicorns such as —Wise, UiPath, Revolut, and Synthesia —Carlos is experienced in identifying and supporting founders from the earliest stage and helping them to create the breakout businesses of tomorrow. Carlos is a published author, podcaster and made it onto Forbes Midas List as one of the most influential VC investors in Europe in 2018, 2019, 2020, 2021, 2022 and 2023. In 2021 Carlos and his colleague Reshma received MBE's from Her Majesty the Queen for services to the British Technology Entrepreneurship Ecosystem.

For fun, you might find Carlos out on a hike, maybe on skis, possibly around a campfire, and most likely near some great coffee spots.

You can find him on:
Twitter - @cee
Blog - http://www.carlosespinal.com
LinkedIn - http://uk.linkedin.com/in/carloseduardoespinal

ABOUT THE AUTHOR

AngelList – https://angel.co/cee
Podcast – https://soundcloud.com/seedcamp
Youtube – https://www.youtube.com/c/seedcamp/videos